Negligence

What Principals Need to Know About Avoiding Liability

Todd A. DeMitchell

ROWMAN & LITTLEFIELD EDUCATION
Lanham • New York • Toronto • Plymouth, UK

ROWMAN & LITTLEFIELD PUBLISHERS, INC.
Published in the United States of America
by Rowman & Littlefield Publishers, Inc.
A wholly owned subsidiary of
The Rowman & Littlefield Publishing Group, Inc.
4501 Forbes Boulevard, Suite 200, Lanham, Maryland 20706
www.rowmanlittlefield.com

Estover Road, Plymouth PL6 7PY
United Kingdom

British Library Cataloguing in Publication Information Available

Library of Congress Cataloging-in-Publication Data

DeMitchell, Todd A.
Negligence : what principals need to know about avoiding liability / Todd A. DeMitchell.
p. cm.
Includes bibliographical references.
ISBN-13: 978-1-57886-500-0 (cloth : alk. paper)
ISBN-10: 1-57886-500-X (cloth : alk. paper)
1. School principals—Legal status, laws, etc.—United States. 2. Educational law and legislation—United States. 3. Liability for school accidents—United States. I. Title.
KF4133.D46 2006
344.73'075—dc22 2006017949

™ The paper used in this publication meets the minimum requirements of American National Standard for Information Sciences—Permanence of Paper for Printed Library Materials, ANSI/NISO Z39.48-1992.
Manufactured in the United States of America.

Contents

Contents

Foreword

Over the years, the role of the American school principal has changed. Twenty-five years ago, principals were primarily expected to be good building managers. "Budgets, buses, and butts" was their area of expertise. The principal's job was to administer student discipline and keep the school facilities in good order, leaving teachers in sole control of student instruction.

That view has changed. In the educational community at least, the principal is now acknowledged to be the instructional leader of the school. Although the management role is undiminished, the principal is also expected to coordinate the school's curriculum, improve student achievement, and develop strategies for lowering the student dropout rate. In short, today's principal is responsible for cultivating and maintaining a healthy educational environment that is conducive to learning.

Sometimes lost in this transition is the recognition that a healthy educational environment must be—first and foremost—a safe environment. Indeed, no matter how sophisticated a school's instructional strategies may be, the learning environment is substandard unless students are safe and perceive themselves to be safe.

Most principal preparation programs address the principal's responsibility for student safety in an education law course that introduces students to the concept of negligence liability for student injuries. Virtually every education law text discusses this topic. Generally, however, these courses cover negligence only briefly, sandwiching it among the other legal issues that principals confront—special education, constitutional rights of students, tenure and promotion of teachers, and so on. It is not surprising that many new principals feel that their knowledge of negligence law is inadequate.

This is unfortunate, because principals are daily required to make important decisions about student safety with no time for reflection or consulting an attorney. Obviously, most principals would make better decisions about student safety if they were knowledgeable about negligence law, particularly as it applies in the school environment.

Fortunately, in *Negligence: What Principals Need to Know About Avoiding Liability*, Todd DeMitchell presents principals and students studying to be principals with a new and comprehensive resource on the topic of negligence. The book clearly explains the law of tort liability and the legal defenses to it, illustrating the legal points with real-life court cases that have arisen in the schools. Professor DeMitchell was a long-time school administrator before he became an education law scholar, and his practical, "in-the-trenches" experience is evident as he explains legal concepts in a way that is meaningful and relevant for principals in their day-to-day school experiences.

In addition, this book is a rich repository of case studies—brief narratives that illustrate the typical kinds of situations that arise in the schools every day. As several case study scholars have pointed out, good case studies provide a bridge between the world of theory and the world of practice (Kowalski, 2004; Merseth, 1997). Certainly, the cases in this book have that quality, illustrating the theoretical principles of negligence law in the context of the everyday reality of the public schools.

Each of these case studies drives home the point that both a moment's thoughtlessness and long inattention by an educator can lead to a student's injury or death. Thus, case by case, the book challenges the reader to reflect on the consequences of carelessness in the schools not only in terms of liability and litigation but also in terms of the lives and well-being of students.

Richard Fossey, J.D., Ed.D.
Professor of Education Law
University of North Texas
Denton, Texas

REFERENCES

Kowalski, T. J. (2004). *Case studies on educational administration*. Boston: Allyn & Bacon.

Merseth, K. K. (1997). *Cases in educational administration*. Boston: Allyn & Bacon.

Acknowledgments

Terri DeMitchell, my wife, has unfailingly encouraged and supported my work. For this project she contributed a chapter, read the entire manuscript a number of times, offered advice. Her perspective as a former elementary school teacher and a former school law attorney has been invaluable in developing this manuscript particularly and my other research generally. All things are possible for me with her by my side.

I dedicate this manuscript to our parents, Bill (my father), Rose (Terri's mother), who are a constant source of support, and in loving memory of Mary (my mother) and Bill (Terri's father).

Preface: On Being a Principal

I wasn't prepared but I felt that I was ready. Is anyone really prepared for his or her first principalship? I had served as an elementary school teacher, lead teacher, and assistant principal, and I had finished my doctorate at a major research university the year before. But was I really prepared? If not, when would I be prepared?

When I first sat behind the desk in my new office I felt exhilarated, daunted, and dared by the responsibility I had assumed for 650 K-8 students and my responsibility for assisting the faculty and staff in providing not just an adequate education but also an excellent education. Curriculum, instruction, evaluation, assessment, bus schedules, procedures for admitting students, supplies, grounds, custodial services, public relations, and communications: the list of things to do and know was long and would get longer as the years progressed and I began to discover all that I did not know.

One thing that I did know was that a safe school for students, faculty, and staff is not just necessary—it is critical. As the leader of the school it is my responsibility to provide and plan for that safety. My introduction to school law sparked an interest in how legal mechanisms impact schools, which served me well as a school administrator, but it has also has been my constant companion that I study, write about, and teach. As I prepared for my first faculty meeting and after reviewing the Faculty Handbook, I actually started writing this book. I knew I needed to be explicit about the importance of providing a safe environment for children and adults. I added a section in the Faculty Handbook on supervision and placed the topic on the agenda for the first meeting. I wanted to be clear that this was a priority.

My first acts as a principal occurred on another coast and in an earlier century, but I continue to believe that safety and security should be a core value of a school. It is a beginning point for all other educational activities. The appropriate discharge of the duty that we owe to our students and our colleagues does not occur by itself. It must be planned for and become part of the way we think about school activities. Knowledge forms habits of mind that lead to habits of action. The goal behind avoiding liability is to provide a safe environment as a habit of mind and a habit of action.

I

INTRODUCTION AND RESEARCH

1

Introduction

> [T]he right of all students to a school environment fit for learning cannot be questioned. Attendance is mandatory and the aim of all schools is to teach. Teaching and learning cannot take place without the physical and mental well-being of the students. The school premises, in short, must be safe and welcoming. . . . (Leger v. Stockton Unified School District)[1]

All too often students are injured at school. If educators take reasonable steps some of the injuries can be prevented. However, some injuries are unforeseen, and no reasonable precautions can prevent them. I begin the discussion of identifying and avoiding potential liability by presenting two real situations where educators could have taken reasonable steps to reduce the likelihood of serious injury but failed to do so, resulting in serious consequences for students.

PUBLIC HIGH SCHOOL IN LOS ANGELES

After eating lunch, two students became involved in a slap boxing match outside the gymnasium. They continued slap boxing for five to ten minutes while a crowd of about thirty students gathered to watch. Suddenly, after being slapped, Michael Daily fell backwards, fracturing his skull on the asphalt paving. He died that night.

Three administrators and two teachers were assigned to supervise 2,700 students during the lunch period. However, the area around the gymnasium was the specific responsibility of the physical education department. The physical education department did not have a formal supervision schedule assigning supervision times and personnel. Instead, supervision was left to the person in the gym office. On the day that Michael Daily died, the chair of the department was playing bridge in the dressing room. The "person in the gym office" sat with his back to the window that looked out on the area outside the gymnasium while talking on the phone, eating his lunch, and preparing for classes. He never turned around to look out the window, nor did he get up to supervise the assigned area.[2]

A PRIVATE ELEMENTARY SCHOOL IN ST. LOUIS

In a Catholic school in St. Louis, a second-grade teacher lit a candle in May in honor of Mary, the Mother of Jesus. The teacher placed the uncovered candle on her desk and never gave her students any warnings or safety instructions about it. One spring afternoon the classroom was alive with excitement. The students were hurriedly changing into costumes for a play rehearsal. The teacher was attending to students, and parents were part of the bustle. Suddenly a shrill cry rang out above the din. The teacher whirled around and, to her horror, saw one of her students engulfed in flames. Her bluebird costume had brushed against the lit candle.[3]

One student died, and another student suffered severe burns and underwent numerous painful surgeries. In both cases educators were sued and found negligent. Unfortunately, these are not isolated events. This book poses case studies, discusses the elements of a tort for negligence, and provides practical suggestions for providing a safe school. It is intended as a refresher for principals and as a resource for those educators who are interested in the duty they owe students. It can also be used as a supplement in school law and principalship classes. The book is organized into five sections: introduction and research, three case studies, a discussion of tort liability and its defenses, specific applications of tort liability, and appendixes that can support recommendations for practice and provide an inservice for principals and/or teachers. It is not, nor should it be considered, a substitute for competent legal advice about the specifics of your school. Competent legal advice can help prudent administrators fashion appropriate responses to their state laws and local conditions. While the principles of negligence are founded on common law, state statutory law structures torts. This requires principals to seek how the principles of tort liability are applied in their state.

NOTES

1. 202 Cal.App. 3d 1448, 1459 (1988).
2. Daily v. Los Angles Unified School District, 470 P. 2d 360 (1970).
3. Smith v. Archbishop of St. Louis, 632 S.W.2d 516 (1982).

2

Research on Liability and the Principal

Principals perform myriad duties in any given day. Curriculum development, instructional supervision, scheduling, planning, community and parental relations, to name just a few, lay important claims on a principal's time. The daily crush of leading and managing a school is complex and demanding. Often, there is not enough time available to research and learn all of the various responsibilities that shape the work of educating students. One such area that is often given short shrift is the legal responsibilities of educators. While much of the work of the principal has a legal dimension, "progress towards educating educators about the law seems slow."[1] Kallio and Valdez found that educators nationwide do not feel that they know enough about the laws governing the educational process.[2]

Because educators are members of a learned profession, and principals generally must take school law as part of the state certification process, a claim of ignorance of the law is an excuse not easily tolerated or accepted by the courts (*ignorantia legis neminem excusat*—ignorance of the law excuses no one). "It is at the school building level that the policies of the school board and the laws governing education are most often implemented. It is also at the school building level that most of the litigation involving school systems begins."[3] This is the beginning point, the school and its principal.

The standard of conduct that principals must meet in the discharge of their professional duties to students is an area not discussed enough. School law is a critical knowledge base for principals.[4] For example, at the national level, the Interstate School Leaders Licensure Consortium (ISLLC) Standard 3 reads: "A school administrator is an educational leader who promotes the success of all students by ensuring management of the organization, operations, and resources for a safe, efficient, and effective learning environment"—this requires knowledge of "legal issues impacting school operations."[5]

One legal issue that impacts the work of principals is the potential liability for negligent behavior of teachers, staff, or the principal himself or herself. Even though principals typically take a school law class that covers negligence, the knowledge gained does not always stay with the principal and become part of the principal's habits of mind and habits of action.

For example, DeMitchell and Carroll's study of principals and negligence found that only 55 percent of the responding principals agreed or strongly agreed that their knowledge of tort liability was sufficient to effectively meet the responsibilities of the principalship, and 72 percent believed that they needed more information about tort liability in order to better perform their job.[6] However, the principals in the study answered 81 percent of the questions correctly on a negligence quiz. (The quiz is placed in a sidebar at the end of this chapter. You are encouraged to take the quiz and to retake it at the end of chapter 13. Answers to the quiz are found in appendix H.)

The principals were first asked: I consider my concern about tort liability/negligence in my school to be: insignificant (1), small (2), medium (3), large (4), or significant (5). Only 16 percent of the respondents considered negligence to be an insignificant or small problem at their school, with 84 percent considering negligence to be a medium to significant problem. The mean score for all principals is 3.4, almost midway between medium and large. It is interesting that middle school principals showed the greatest concern over negligence, with 65.5 percent considering it to be a large or significant issue (mean 3.6).

The second question ("My superintendent stresses the importance of the issue of tort liability to the principals.") tried to gauge the impact that superintendents have on principals' perception of the importance of tort liability. Below are the question and the responses from principals.

Table 2.1

Level (N=)	*1 Strongly Disagree*	*2 Disagree*	*3 Neutral*	*4 Agree*	*5 Strongly Agree*	*Mean*
Elem (21)	0 0%	3 14.3%	4 19.0%	13 61.9%	1 4.8%	3.6 (.79)
Middle (29)	2 6.9%	2 6.9%	7 24.1%	14 48.3%	4 13.8%	3.6 (1.04)
High (32)	0 0%	3 9.4%	15 46.9%	7 21.9%	7 21.9%	3.6 (1.00)
Total (82)	2 2.4%	2.4% 9.8%	8 31.7%	9.8% 41.5%	26 14.6%	1.7% (.94)

While all of the means are the same, there is variability between the levels. The elementary school principals had less variability (s.d .79) than the middle (s.d. 1.04) and high school (s.d. 1.00) principals. Fifty-six percent agree or strongly agree with the statement. A Pearson Product Moment correlation between questions 1 and 2 shows a moderate positive correlation ($r = .372$).[7] In other words, there is a moderate relationship between the stress placed on tort liability by the superintendent and the degree of significance the principal ascribes to the issue of tort liability.

A partial explanation for why the correlation is not stronger may be found in the surprising 32 percent neutral response, meaning possibly that the principals may not know where their superintendent stands on this issue. This question raises a concern as to how seriously superintendents take the issue of tort liability and whether superintendents discuss the issue with their principals. It can be argued that the superintendent sets the agenda for what gets done and what gets paid attention to. If superintendents don't incorporate a concern for tort liability in daily decision making, will their principals incorporate it? If superintendents want principals to be proactive about avoiding liability and protecting individuals within the schools, they must communicate its importance.

Principals in the study considered tort liability to be a medium concern. How many lawsuits and potential lawsuits have principals faced that may impact their perception of the magnitude of the issue? The respondents were asked several questions regarding the number of lawsuits they faced in the last five years.

In the last five years how many times has your school been threatened with a lawsuit for tort liability/negligence?

None	One Time	Two to Five Times	More Than Five Times
48	12	19	1

More high school principals report threats of lawsuits (fifteen) than middle school principals (twelve) and elementary school principals (five). School districts with more than five thousand students report more threats of lawsuits than smaller school districts. Urban school districts report more threats than town/suburban school districts or rural school districts.

In the last five years how many times has your school been served with legal papers bringing a lawsuit for tort liability/negligence?

None	One Time	Two to Five Times	More Than Five Times
60	13	5	1

High school principals reported the most papers being served (eleven versus six for middle school principals and two for elementary school principals). Only high school principals and one middle school principal reported being served papers two to five times and more than five times.

In the last five years how many times has your school had to defend itself in court for a suit for tort liability/negligence?

None	One Time	Two to Five Times	More Than Five Times
70	4	3	0

Four high school principals and one middle school principal reported one instance of defending themselves in court. Three high school principals reported two to five instances of court action requiring a defense. Urban high schools appear to be greater targets than other combinations of type and location.[8]

The survey also sought to find out how principals reduced their and the school's exposure to liability. Thirty-two percent of the principals stated that they had included sections in their faculty handbook covering tort liability. Of the 32 percent who included sections in the faculty handbook, more middle school principals (46 percent) reported including a tort liability section in their faculty handbook than high school principals (25 percent) or elementary school principals (23 percent). Seventy-three percent stated that they discussed liability at least once a year with their faculty. This is almost the inverse of the number of principals who had sections in their handbook. Whether these discussions were informal or had a definite script with articulated principles is unknown.

In my estimation, informal conversations are not sufficient for building knowledge about tort liability and a concern for liability, and for building habits of action, which increase safety. A policy provides a consistent basis upon which to base actions. It is also an authoritative statement of the importance of providing a safe environment. I strongly encourage principals to include sections in their faculty handbooks on the expectations of supervision. Appendix B provides a sample handbook policy. You are encouraged to use it and modify it to meet the special needs and circumstances of your school.

The importance of a principal's knowledge about negligence is underscored by the number of lawsuits filed and by the size of the award mean in school negligence cases. The mean award is $1,073,890, with an award median of $100,000 within an award range between $1 and $105,000,000.[9] Further, the University of California at Los Angeles Cyberspace Law & Policy Center report on a survey of five hundred public school districts revealed that during a three-year period students filed 1,047 lawsuits and 821 (78.4 percent) were based on allegations of negligence.[10]

Lawsuits are costly in terms of money, time, and emotional energy. For the injured, their pain and suffering can be incalculable. Teachers and principals are drawn to education because it is one of the oldest helping professions. Acts that result in injury to their students can have devastating effects on educators and impact the climate of the school. Teachers and principals make decisions at a fast clip—day in and day out—that create potential harm and resulting liability. The imperative of leadership compels principals to act. Since these decisions are made without the benefit of legal advice, it is imperative that educators—particularly principals, as leaders of their schools—have a firm grasp of the basics of tort liability.

This quiz was given to the principals in the DeMitchell and Carroll study. Please take the quiz at this time and retake it at the end of the final chapter. You can compare your scores for changes and then check your pretest and posttest scores with the answers in appendix H .

PRETEST ON TORT LIABILITY

TRUE or FALSE

1. T F Educators owe a legal duty to their students.
2. T F The reasonable person concept applies to educators under tort liability/negligence.
3. T F Principals cannot be held liable when a teacher's act or failure to act causes an injury.
4. T F Proximate cause is a defense in tort liability/negligence cases.
5. T F As the foreseeability of injury increases so must the duty owed increase.
6. T F Breach of duty is an aspect of the prima facie case in tort liability issues.
7. T F Sufficient injury or actual loss or injury must be proved in tort liability/negligence cases.
8. T F Adequate/proper supervision is an aspect of the duty eductors owe their students.
9. T F All torts involve negligence.

(percentage of questions answered correctly by the principals: all: 81.1%; elementary: 78.3%; middle: 83.1%; high: 81.3%)

NOTES

1. Sarah E. Redfield (2002), *The Convergence of Education and Law: A New Class of Educators and Lawyers.* Paper Presentation, Education Law Association, New Orleans, LA at 6.

2. Brenda Kallio and Liliana Valdez (2002), *Sources and Effectiveness of Legal Training for Educational Administrators.* Paper Presentation, Education Law Association, New Orleans, LA at 5.

3. Gerald C. Ubben, Larry W. Hughes, and Cynthia J. Norris, *The Principal: Creative Leadership for Excellence in Schools,* 344 (5th ed. 2004).

4. David J. Sperry, *Working in a Legal and Regulatory Environment: A Handbook for School Leaders* (1999).

5. Council of Chief State School Officers, *Interstate School Leaders Licensure Consortium: Standards for School Leaders* (1996).

6. Todd A. DeMitchell and Thomas J. Carroll (2004), *Negligence and Students: Issues, Response, and Knowledge (Tort Liability and the Public School Principal)*. Paper Presentation, Education Law Association, Tucson, AZ. Also *see*, Scott S. Brabrand (2003), *Virginia Principals and School Law*. Unpublished doctoral dissertation, Virginia Polytechnic Institute and State University, Blacksburg, VA. His study concluded that Virginia principals had an "adequate knowledge of tort liability with an average score of 72.9%" at 62.

7. *Thomas Urdan Statistics in Plain English* (2001). (0 to .2 weak; .2 to .5 moderate; .5 and above strong.)

8. A study of principals and tort liability found 25 percent of those responding had lawsuits or out-of-court settlements in the last two years. (American Tort Reform Association, "School Principal Survey Reveals Fear of Liability Limits Educational Opportunities for America's Children." Site visited 12/8/05, http://www.atra.org/show/91.)

9. Rachel Kaiman (Ed.), *School Negligence and Safety Claims: An Inside Look at Limiting Your School's Exposure*, 5 (2003).

10. Stuart Biegel, "K-12 Campus Safety: A Legal Perspective." Site visited 2/13/05, www.gseis.ucla.edu/iclp/safety.htm, at 1–2.

II

CASE STUDIES

3

Case Studies

The following three case studies are intended to give the reader the opportunity to apply the principles of tort liability for negligence to situations that are encountered in the elementary, middle, and high school. Guiding questions are posed so that the reader can develop answers prior to reading about tort liability and then check them for accuracy after reading the book. Principals and superintendents can also use these case studies for inservice opportunities with teachers and administrators. Responses to the questions are found in appendix A.

RECESS DUTY AT THE SWINGS: ELEMENTARY SCHOOL SCENARIO

Mr. Roberts, a second-grade teacher, is scheduled for recess duty with grades one through three at the swings and monkey bars. He lines his students up for recess but he does not follow them to the playground and then to his duty station. Instead, he goes to the lounge to get a cup of coffee and ends up chatting for a couple of minutes with a few of the teachers. It is not that Mr. Roberts deliberately avoids his recess duty; he just doesn't give it much thought. He considers it more of a chore and an inconvenience than a professional obligation. He has never refused to go to his duty station, and he has not complained openly to the principal about standing duty, but he has missed an occasional duty and has been noticeably late a number of times.

When he finally arrives at the duty station, approximately eight minutes late for his fifteen-minute duty, he finds a large group of students gathered around the swings. Pushing through the crowd, he finds a student lying motionless on the ground in a contorted position. He quickly ascertains that the child has been seriously injured by a fall after shinnying up the legs of the swing support to the crossbar.

Guiding Questions

1. Would a reasonable teacher go to the lounge for a cup of coffee instead of going directly to the assigned duty?
2. Would Mr. Roberts's duty increase if the teachers had specific knowledge that the injured student had a propensity to climb the swing set?
3. If there is another teacher on duty and that teacher notices that Mr. Roberts is not on duty, has the duty of that teacher increased to encompass the swing set?
4. If the principal knows that Mr. Roberts has the history stated above, can the principal be liable for negligent supervision if he or she does not take appropriate steps regarding Mr. Roberts?

A FIELD TRIP TO THE SEASHORE: MIDDLE SCHOOL SCENARIO

Two seventh-grade students drowned while on a field trip to the seashore. Both students had been showing off in front of the class for about fifteen minutes before they wandered away from the class. They had been gone for about forty-five minutes before they were discovered missing. It was determined later that the two students had been pulled out to sea by an undertow, where they subsequently drowned.

Signed permission slips to attend the field trip had been returned by all of the students except one—one of the students who drowned. The principal was aware of the lack of a signed permission slip but relented when the student pleaded with her. Of the two teachers assigned to the sixty-five students, one became ill the day of the field trip and could not attend. The principal assigned a student teacher to take the regular teacher's place. The student teacher was said to be "mature" for his age. However, since the trip took place in late September, the student teacher had been with one of the classes for only two weeks and had no solo teaching experience. There were no other adults assigned as chaperones.

After arriving at the seashore the students were instructed one time, prior to getting off the bus, to stay close to the group, not to wander off, and to be careful. No other directions were given and no tally of the number of students was made at any time. The seashore had several rocky projections that were screened from the view from the beach. Once behind the projections, a person could not be easily seen from the beach. It was behind one of these rocky outcroppings that the students congregated and were either swept out sea or decided to go swimming. It was there that the students died.

Guiding Questions:

1. What steps should the principal have taken regarding the field trip to the seashore?
2. What steps should the teacher have taken while on the bus and after letting the students off the bus?
3. How did the seashore increase the duty owed to the students?
4. How is time important to this case study?

MS. SMITH'S VERY BAD DAY: HIGH SCHOOL SCENARIO

Ms. Smith, by all accounts, was a very good teacher. She taught her chemistry classes with style and enthusiasm. She planned thoroughly, cared about her students' achievement, and conducted her classes in a lively, engaging manner. She comported herself in a professional manner. Ms. Smith was indeed a very good chemistry teacher, but one day . . .

Ms. Smith forgot to set her alarm clock ahead with the shift to daylight savings time. Consequently, she was late to work on that first Monday. Her first-period chemistry class was milling outside her classroom door. Mr. Owens, the principal, was looking at his watch with a perturbed countenance when Ms. Smith finally arrived through the side door. She quickly ushered her students inside and made a quick apology to Mr. Owens.

Normally Ms. Smith had her science experiments set up before the students arrived. But since she was late she did not have this preparation completed. While she quickly set up the experiment, she told her class to review the experiment procedures for the day as found in the text. The unit test was scheduled for later in the week and the material needed to be covered. She hastily set out the needed chemicals, including the caustic chemicals. Slightly out of breath when the last station was prepared, she called out to the class, "Are there any questions?" She was greeted with silence, and three seconds later she told them to go to their stations and begin.

Ms. Smith then walked to her desk and busily perused her plans for the rest of the day. She became engrossed in her plans and did not get up or look up from her desk for five minutes. Suddenly her concentration was broken by a terrified scream: "My eyes, they burn!" She turned to see Steve frantically clawing his eyes while his lab partner was leading him to the emergency eye wash station. She immediately noticed that Steve did not have on his safety goggles as required when working with caustic chemicals. In fact, almost half of the students were not wearing their goggles. Ms. Smith always warned students to wear their goggles and would not allow experiments to begin until all students had their goggles securely in place. The textbook also warned students to wear their goggles when performing this particular experiment. Steve was one of the students that she often had to remind to wear his goggles and would direct him to not take them off until she told the class that it was acceptable to take them off. Steve would often not put on his goggles and/or he would remove them before Ms. Smith gave the go-ahead to safely remove them. Steve always complained that the goggles gave him goggle hair, which lasted all day after chemistry class.

Guiding Questions:

1. Did Ms. Smith owe an increased duty to Steve?
2. Was Steve's injury foreseeable?
3. Would Ms. Smith be liable if she had instructed the students to wear their goggles and after she checked and turned away from Steve he took his goggles off and immediately got the caustic chemicals in his eyes?
4. The textbook provides a warning about wearing goggles. Is that sufficient to relieve Ms. Smith of liability?

III

TORT LIABILITY AND ITS DEFENSES

4

Tort Liability

Lawsuits alleging that educators committed an act of negligence are a part of the educational landscape. In fact, the threat of lawsuits has become so commonplace that elementary school children have been heard to say that they are going to sue the teacher or the principal. These threats are real and they impact the work of educators. They often prompt educators to act in a prudent fashion, but sometimes they paralyze educators into inaction or defensive teaching. Educators work with the specter of being sued constantly hovering over their shoulder. But what constitutes a lawsuit alleging negligence?

The law of torts is concerned with the allocation of losses arising out of human activities. The word *tort* is derived from the Latin word *tortus*, which means twisted.[1] In common use it is a synonym for the word *wrong*. The purpose of the law of torts is to adjust these losses, and to afford compensation for injuries sustained by one person as the result of the conduct of another. "Broadly speaking, a tort is a civil wrong, other than breach of contract, for which the court will provide a remedy in the form of an action for damages."[2] If someone suffers a harm or loss due to the improper conduct of another, a tort may have been committed. A tort is an action brought by an individual. It is not a criminal action. However, actions that give rise to the tort, such as assault and battery, may also constitute a crime.

For example, the former football player O. J. Simpson was tried for murder by the state of California. He was also sued for the tort of wrongful death by the parents of one of the murder victims. Simpson was found not guilty in the murder case but was found liable for wrongful death. The finding of liability resulted in a damage award to the parents of the victim. The facts were essentially the same, but the trials were independent of each other, using their respective rules of evidence and standards of proof.[3]

The law of torts is primarily judge fashioned (arising out of court cases) and is grounded in the concept of fault.[4] It applies to individuals who cause a car crash or leave a roller skate where a visitor slips on it, and it applies to entities, such as supermarkets, that do not clean up liquid spills in their aisles in a timely fashion. As individuals, we can be held accountable for our actions or failure to act under certain circumstances. The same is true of school districts.

Torts are usually divided into three categories: (1) negligence, (2) intentional torts,[5] and (3) strict liability.[6] This discussion will focus on the tort of negligence. The discussion is further limited in that constitutional torts in which public school officials can be held liable for the violation of a person's constitutional or federal statutory rights will not be discussed.[7]

"Negligence is generally the omission or failure to do something that a reasonable person would do, or the doing of something that a reasonable person would not do."[8] Stated more specifically, negligence is defined as a breach of one's legal duty to protect others against unreasonable risks of harm.[9] The act is unintentional. In order to prevail in a tort for negligence, the plaintiff must prove the four elements of a tort: (1) there was a duty owed by defendant to plaintiff; a duty to conform to a specific standard of conduct; (2) the duty was breached by the defendant; failure to conform to the standard required; (3) the defendant's conduct was the actual and proximate cause of plaintiff's injury; and (4) actual damage to plaintiff resulted.[10]

DUTY OWED

As a general rule, a person has no affirmative duty to aid or protect another. However, there are situations when a duty may be owed to another. A public school educator's relationship to his or her student is one of those relationships in which one party (the educator) owes a duty to the other party (the student). In addition, a school board, like any landowner, "has an obligation to use reasonable care to maintain its property in a physically safe condition."[11]

"[A] child while in school is deprived of the protection of his parents or guardians. Therefore, the actor who takes custody is properly required to give him the protection which the custody or manner in which it is taken has deprived him."[12] "The duty owed derives from the simple fact that a school, in assuming physical custody and control over its students, effectively takes the place of parents and guardians"[13] Since teachers stand in loco parentis (custodial and tutelary responsibilities),[14] they must take affirmative actions in the face of foreseeable risks to protect students. "Duty requires the exercise of care for protection against *unreasonable* risks of harm."[15]

> The usual relationship between student and school is that the child must attend school and obey school rules. Students under the control and protection of the school are thus not able to protect themselves. The protective custody of teachers is substituted for that of the parents. (Travis v. Bohannon)[16]

Factors relevant in determining whether a duty exists include the foreseeability of injury, the likelihood of injury, the magnitude of the burden of guarding against the injury, the consequences of placing that burden on the defendant, and the possible seriousness of the injury.[17] Whether a specific duty exists is a question of law to be determined by the court; a duty is not created by its mere allegation asserted by a plaintiff.[18] But, do educators owe a duty of due care to their students? The answer is unequivocally yes.

There is no one set of standards for defining the duty that is owed by educators. Since tort liability, with the exception of constitutional torts, which will not be discussed, is a state action, the various states define the duty owed differently. For example, the uniform standard of care owed to students in California is that degree of care "which a person of ordinary prudence, charged with [comparable] duties, would exercise under the same circumstances."[19] New Hampshire educators owe their students a duty of reasonable supervision because schools share a special relationship with students entrusted to their care.[20] In Mississippi, "educators have the duty of exercising ordinary care, . . . or of acting as a reasonable person would act under similar circumstances."[21] In Kansas, the duty is "to properly supervise students and to take reasonable steps to protect students' safety."[22]

Students are compelled to attend school. This compulsion helps to form the common law duty as well as statutory duty, supported by case law, to anticipate foreseeable dangers and to take necessary precautions to protect students. Educators owe students a duty to "exercise such care of them as a parent of ordinary prudence would observe in comparable circumstances. The duty owed derives from the simple fact that a school, in assuming physical custody and control over its students, effectively takes the place of parents and guardians."[23] Mandatory schooling forces parents to rely on schools to protect their children during school activities.[24]

For example, a suit was brought against a school district for injuries sustained when a first grader tripped over a crack in the playground while playing tag. The court found for the defendant school district stating that the school exercised "the same degree of care and supervision of [the child] that a reasonably prudent parent would employ in the given circumstances."[25] Similarly, a teacher was on hall duty when a plaintiff seventh grader was running in the hall. He did not stop running when the teacher told him to stop running. As the student ran past the teacher, the teacher stuck out his leg and tripped the student. The student sued for negligent supervision and won. The court stated that the standard of care is that supervision that a parent of ordinary prudence would undertake in comparable circumstances. Finding the teacher liable, the court asserted that a parent of ordinary prudence would not have tried to stop a child from running past by sticking out his leg.[26]

Schools do not owe a duty to their students in all situations. An example of when a school does not owe a duty to students is found in the state of Washington. An appellate court held that school officials did not have a duty to supervise students participating in a senior "release" day.[27] School personnel had knowledge of the event, but they neither planned nor attended the event. It was not a school-sponsored event, even though it involved students at the school.

Similarly, once a student leaves the control of the school, the duty typically ends unless it is a school-sponsored trip or a school-associated activity.[28] An example of egregious conduct perpetrated by a teacher against one of his students is found in New York. A high school social studies teacher was convicted of the statutory rape of a fifteen-year-old student. The sexual contact took place off school grounds "beyond the scope of Barsky's employment as a teacher and when the plaintiff was not within the school's control."[29] The court reasoned that the school did not have custody of the female student at the time of the assaults.

"Without custody of the child, the school has no duty; without a duty there can be no liability."[30]

While schools typically owe a duty to students who are under their supervision, they do not insure the safety of the students.[31] For example, in *Brownell*, a student was shot while standing in front of the school just after school hours by a nonstudent gang member.[32] The court held that schools couldn't insure the safety of students, particularly after or before school hours and off school premises.[33] Similarly, a student was seriously injured when he ran back to the highway to retrieve papers he had dropped after exiting the school bus. The Idaho court held that the school owed no duty to the student at the time of the accident. It had fulfilled its duty by seeing him to the driveway of his house.[34]

OBLIGATIONS OF AN EDUCATOR

The duty that educators owe students is often phrased as "obligations" in the professional literature. These obligations typically involve three activities: (1) providing adequate supervision; (2) providing proper instructions; and (3) providing properly maintained buildings, grounds, and equipment. The fourth obligation of an educator spans all three obligations—providing warnings regarding known or reasonably foreseeable hazards.[35]

An allegation of failure to provide adequate supervision for students is perhaps the most common negligence claim.[36] The gym, playground, and athletic activities account for 49 percent of the places where negligent supervision is reported.[37] "Constant and unremitting vigilance and supervision are not required. What is always required, however, is the care that a reasonable and prudent person would take in the circumstances."[38] The level of supervision required varies with the circumstances surrounding the supervision. Such factors as the age and maturity of the students, the prior knowledge about the students and/or situation, and the nature of the specific activity are all-important considerations. For example, working with first graders in the classroom or outside the classroom generally requires a higher level of supervision than that provided to high school students. In at least one jurisdiction, the courts have held that the playground is "a place where close supervision of the children is all but mandatory."[39]

Similarly, if high school students are using a trampoline, the degree of supervision owed to the students increases dramatically because the risk of foreseeable harm has increased. Obviously, being involved in the chemistry lab, the woodshop, and many athletic activities such as swimming and gymnastics call for a greater degree of vigilance and more specific supervision on the part of the educator than regular classroom instruction.

In one case, the level of the duty owed was heightened because the defendant school was a boarding school. The Oregon Appellate Court held that a special relationship was created with the student, which required the school to properly supervise the visits of the student's father. The father raped his daughter.[40]

Another issue associated with supervising students is the presence of the teacher during student activities. Must the teacher be present at all times? Can a teacher be absent for good reasons? These are questions that I often receive when I teach school law. My response is to look at the activity the students are involved in and what the teacher knows about the students. A good rule of thumb to use when analyzing teacher absence is found in the following court case.

Proper Supervision and Absence from the Classroom

A teacher was found negligent when he left approximately fifty junior high school students unsupervised for approximately twenty-five minutes. *Cirillo v. City of Milwaukee* listed several considerations when viewing a suit that alleges that the teacher negligently supervised his or her classroom by being absent when the injury occurred.

1. What activity were the students engaged in when the teacher left the classroom?
2. What instruments were the students working with when the teacher left the classroom (band saw, dangerous chemicals, pencils, etc.)?
3. What is the age and composition of the class?
4. What is the teacher's past experience with the class and its propensities?
5. What is the reason for and the duration of the teacher's absence?[41]

An area of supervision that is receiving increased scrutiny is bullying. "Bullying has been linked, among other activities, to factors that have resulted in violence at school. Bullying can contribute to an environment of fear and intimidation."[42] Both boys and girls bully. Boys tend to bully both boys and girls, while girls tend to primarily choose girls. Girls are more likely to bully in groups. Bullying tends to increase through elementary grades, peak in middle school, and drop off by eleventh and twelfth grades.[43]

The issue for principals is whether they are providing adequate supervision and responding to instances of bullying. The National Center for Educational Statistics publication *Indicators of School Crime and Safety* underscores the extent of the problem. In 2003, 7 percent of students ages twelve to eighteen reported they had been bullied during the last six months.[44] Sixth-grade students show the highest reported instances of bullying in a six-month period (14 percent of the students).

Children often push, shove, bump, tease, and otherwise aggravate each other. While many of these behaviors are done without thinking and not calculated to inflict harm, bullying has a different quality to the actions. A bully is conscious of the impact of his or her behavior; the behavior is willful and calculated. While the behavior of the bully is not negligent, it is intentional, and principals may be negligent in their response to bullying behavior.

> Four elements are invariably present in bullying: (1) an imbalance of power, where the bully is bigger, stronger, or more favorably situated than the victim, e.g., more popular or more accepted by peers; (2) a purposeful intent to harm, physically or emotionally; (3) the threat of future aggression; and (4) the victim's unremitting terror, agitation or fear. (Kathleen Conn, Ph.D., J.D., LL.M., principal, East Lansdowne Basic School, Lansdowne, PA)[45]

Responses to bullying have involved state legislation[46] as well as lawsuits. Principals are advised to review their state laws for a statutorily directed duty owed to victims of bullying. While the number of state laws has increased to twenty-three states, there is concern that the laws are not effective.[47] Therefore, parents and their children may be resorting to litigation for a redress of inadequate supervision of bullies.[48]

The duty of adequate supervision is not confined to supervising students. Principals must also supervise adults, including teachers, custodians, and other school employees. In the last several years, attorneys, filing lawsuits against school districts for the negligent supervision of employees, contacted me about their cases. In one case, the plaintiff student alleged that the principal inadequately supervised the special education teacher and the classroom instructional aide. The claim asserted that the principal's failure to adequately supervise the adults led to the adults inadequately supervising two students during a bathroom break, which resulted in the sexual assault of the kindergarten-aged student by a known aggressive student. In the second case, a teacher alleged that a custodian was improperly supervised. The custodian allegedly harassed, stalked, and threatened to kill the teacher and her family. The plaintiff argued that the administration, the principal, and the superintendent failed to adequately supervise the custodian, who had been moved twice to different schools. And, their failure resulted in an injury.

DUTY OWED BY PRINCIPALS AND SUPERINTENDENTS

> The superintendent and the principal are charged with the overall operation of the school. Therefore, a duty of supervision is owed to all students. Where the "principal or superintendent knows or should know that a particular employee poses a threat to a student, entrustment of the student to the care of that employee will not satisfy the duty of reasonable supervision."[49]

Proper instructions are necessary to reduce the risk of injury when a student undertakes an activity, especially a dangerous activity. A chemistry lab is a prime location where inadequate instructions or failure to warn a student of known or foreseeable dangers has led to successful claims of negligence. For example, a teacher was held liable for failing to warn and instruct students about the use of methanol around a flame.[50]

To just give an instruction once is probably not enough if there is an ongoing foreseeable risk of injury. For example, a successful claim was brought against a field hockey coach. The coach told his players at the beginning of the season to wear their mouth protectors. A sixteen-year-old student was struck in the mouth with a hockey stick. She was not wearing her mouth protector. The coach failed to remind the students to wear their mouth protectors and failed to check to see that the players had their mouth protectors in, which can be readily seen by a quick scan of a player's face. The coach had observed the student for thirty minutes, during which time she did not wear her protector, but took no action.[51]

A physical education teacher directed two students to fight each other as part of an improvised lesson. Neither student had received any instructions in boxing. One student was superior to the other in size, strength, and athletic ability. After giving the students gloves for the fight the teacher sat in the stands and watched the fight, never intervening or giving directions even when it was apparent that the smaller student was getting pummeled. During the second round the smaller student was killed. The teacher was held liable for inadequate supervision and lack of proper instructions.[52]

The third obligation is to properly maintain buildings, grounds, and equipment. Courts will routinely award monetary damages to students who are injured by unsafe conditions that school authorities should have known of and failed to take necessary precautions to reduce the risk of injury. "All school personnel share a common responsibility to keep school facilities reasonably safe."[53] However, not all injuries at school result in a finding of negligence. The issue of notice or constructive notice of a dangerous condition is important.

A fifth-grade student slipped and fell in front of his locker as a result of accumulated water on the floor. In order to sustain a slip and fall action against the school district, the plaintiff had to prove that the school district knew that water had accumulated on the floor or that "defect must be visible and apparent and it must exist for a sufficient time prior to the accident to permit defendant's employees to discover and remedy it."[54] There was no evidence to show that the principal or members of the faculty or staff had knowledge of any water accumulation and therefore no liability was found. At the trial, they specifically stated that they did not see any water in front of the defendant's locker, nor was there a history of a problem of water accumulation in that spot either from rain or snow. However, when a student put his arm through a broken window and was injured, the defendant school district lost because it had allowed the broken window to go unfixed for four months.[55]

In another instance, school district leaders in a Tennessee school were made aware that kitchen workers were receiving electrical shocks "strong enough to 'shock the water . . . out of you'"[56] The defendant school district made four attempts to fix the problems but appeared to want to wait until a large renovation project planned for the near future to fully rectify the situation. Unfortunately, the cafeteria manager received a debilitating shock prior to the major renovation. The plaintiff won at the appellate court level. The school district had been put on notice of a dangerous condition and it failed to remedy the problem.

The last obligation requires the educator to provide warnings regarding known or reasonably foreseeable hazards. This obligation encompasses the three prior obligations and the concept of causation. Basically, if an educator has knowledge of a hazard that can likely cause injury, the educator must take appropriate steps to reduce the risk of injury. For example, if a dangerous situation exists due to construction near the school that may reasonably cause injury to students traveling to and from school, it is prudent to notify parents of the increased risk of harm.

However, courts will pose the question whether the defendant educator knew or should have known about the dangerous condition. Pleading ignorance or turning a blind eye to a potential problem are poor strategies. For example, a student was injured by a snowball and brought a suit for negligent supervision. The court held that the "educators knew or should have known, of hard frozen snow or ice in the school yard that caused the child's injury."[57] Consequently, principals cannot sit back and wait for dangerous conditions to be brought to their attention. They must act with due diligence to keep attuned to potential problem areas in their school. If construction is taking place at the school, courts would expect that the prudent principal would have known of the potential danger and had taken reasonable steps to reduce the likelihood of injury.

BREACH OF DUTY

A breach of duty occurs when the defendant's conduct falls below that required by the standard of care owed to the plaintiff. An important consideration is how the educator discharged or failed to discharge his or her duty. For example, an educator who fails to act properly when there exists a duty to act has acted with misfeasance. Second, an educator who fails to act when required to act has breached his or her duty through nonfeasance. And, last of all, an educator who acts unlawfully and wrongfully breaches the duty owed through malfeasance.

Breach of duty is the application of the facts to the reasonable person standard that demonstrates breach. For example, a shop teacher owes his or her students a duty to provide proper instructions before allowing them to use a welding torch. A student is injured when she uses the torch improperly as directed by the teacher. The teacher's failure to provide the required instructions establishes a breach of duty.

The courts apply a uniform and objective standard of care called the "reasonable person." The reasonable person is a mythical person who is always prudent and careful, not to be identified with any ordinary individual who might occasionally do unreasonable things. The application of the reasonable person standard involves comparing the conduct of the defendant with "what the reasonable person would do 'under the same or similar circumstances.'"[58] This hypothetical reasonable person has (1) the same physical characteristics as the defendant; (2) normal intelligence, problem-solving ability, and temperament; (3) normal perception and memory with a minimum level of information and experience common to the community; and (4) such superior skill and knowledge as the defendant has or purports to have.[59]

In a New York case, a coach was held to the standard of the reasonably prudent coach and not the reasonably prudent parent.[60] This appears to establish a higher standard of reasonableness for educators who have acquired special knowledge and skills. "Teachers, being college graduates and state licensed, are expected to act like reasonable persons with similar education."[61] In the case study "Recess Duty at the Swings" (see chapter 3) the court would ask whether a reasonable teacher would go get a cup of coffee, thus arriving late to recess duty.

Students are also held to the reasonable person standard. For example, a school district sued the mother of an eleven-year-old student for negligence under the theory of vicarious liability. Her son pointed a small (two to three inches long, with the thickness of a dime) toy gun and shouted "bang" at one of its employees. The teacher's assistant claimed that she suffered mental and emotional trauma from the event. The student had an emotional and behavioral disorder and was receiving services in a special education program at the time of the incident. The Court of Appeals for Louisiana stated that the student's action "must be compared to that of a reasonably prudent eleven-year-old boy who has the same exceptionalities as does [the defendant]."[62] In addition, the court held that the maturity level, knowledge of the situation, and the circumstances involved, including awareness of the risks involved, must be gauged against the reasonably prudent eleven-year-old with the defendant's exceptionalities. The court held that the student had not breached the standard of care applicable to him. Therefore, the school district's suit for negligence failed.

In some instances, the educator must have knowledge of the dangerous condition in order to be held responsible. For example, a student was injured when another student shoved a desk that hit the student. For an educator to be liable for injuries caused by the acts of fellow students, the plaintiff in order to establish breach "must show that the [educator] had sufficient specific knowledge or notice of the dangerous conduct which caused the injury."[63] In a New York case, a student was hit in the eye with a stick thrown by another student during lunch recess. The horseplay between the two students that led to the injury lasted approximately one minute. The Supreme Court, Appellate Division, Second Department held that the third-party act of throwing the stick could not have been reasonably anticipated, thus there was no breach.[64] "An injury caused by the impulsive, unanticipated act of a fellow student ordinarily will not give rise to a finding of negligence absent proof of prior conduct that would have put a reasonable person on notice to protect against the injury causing act."[65] In these situations, the courts find that the standard of knew or should have known does not apply because it would be unreasonable for the educator to have anticipated the act.

> School personnel cannot reasonably be expected to guard against all of the sudden spontaneous acts that take place among students. (Mitzel v. New York City Board of Education)[66]

Breach of duty may also be shown by evidence of a statutory violation. For example, a bus driver broke the law when he failed to use his stop sign and lights, which resulted in an injury to a student. His violation of the law constituted a breach of duty.[67]

A school employee threw a number of cans of highly flammable duplicating fluid containing varying amounts of fluid in the Dunn Elementary School's Dumpster during the summer. The school had a significant history of break-ins and vandalism. It was known that students often rummaged in the Dumpsters. Two minors (both over the age of twelve) took four of the cans of partially used duplicating fluid and started some small fires in a nearby housing project. One of individuals returned to the Dumpster for a fifth can and while playing with the fluid created a fireball that struck a student in the chest, causing severe burns to his face and body. The injured student had just turned a corner of the building when he was struck.

The school was cognizant of the risk of harm created by the duplicating fluid because it took special precautions for storage of the fluid.

The school district at the trial explained the purpose of the safeguards. "We were aware of the fact that Dunn School had a history of break-ins and vandalism and we did not want duplicating fluid to be used in setting fires."[68] The school had a duty to properly dispose of the fluid. It knew of the unreasonable risk of harm that duplicating fluid presented to students who knowingly hunted through the school's Dumpster. It was foreseeable and foreseen by the school that unsupervised use of the fluid could cause injuries such as those suffered by the plaintiff. The school did not act reasonably by throwing cans with duplicating fluid still in them in a place that students were known to frequent. Therefore, it breached its duty to the plaintiff.

On occasion, an individual who owes a duty to the injured party injures a person and a specific finding of breach is not possible. In those unique situations the doctrine of *res ipsa loquitur* ("the thing speaks for itself"), although rare, allows a plaintiff to demonstrate breach without a specific factual finding of breach. In certain cases negligence can be inferred from the facts. For example, in *Byrne v. Boadle,*[69] breach was established when a barrel rolled out of a warehouse's second-story window and hit a passerby. The court concluded that barrels do not roll out of windows on their own. Therefore, some unspecified negligent act caused the barrel to roll out the window. This doctrine "spares the plaintiff the requirement of proving specific acts of negligence in cases where the plaintiff asserts . . . injury, the cause of which cannot be fully explained, and the injury is of a type that would not ordinarily result if the defendant were not negligent."[70]

In an education case, *res ipsa loquitur* was applied when a metal-encased frame of glass fell on a student while she was seated in a mobile-unit classroom.[71] Frames of glass do not normally fall out of their frames without some inferred negligence. A New York Court of Appeals in 2004 allowed the plaintiff parent, whose child had multiple handicaps, including cerebral palsy, mental retardation, and quadriplegia, to assert *res ipsa loquitur* against the school board for injuries suffered aboard the school bus.[72]

CAUSATION

Once a duty owed by the defendant to the plaintiff has been established, and the facts demonstrate that the plaintiff breached the duty owed by failing to act as a reasonable person, the plaintiff must next show that the act or failure to act was the cause of the injury. Causation has two elements: cause-in-fact and proximate cause (legal cause). Cause-in-fact is often called the "but-for test," which states that, but for the defendant's conduct, the injury would not have occurred.

The second part of cause-in-fact is the substantial factor test. Under this test, the defendant's conduct is the cause-in-fact if it is substantial enough to lead reasonable persons to conclude that the act caused the injury. The "negligent act must be in continuous and active force up to the actual harm."[73] The term *cause-in-fact* "embraces all things which have so far contributed to the result that without them it would not have occurred."[74] "To make a prima facie showing of [cause-in-fact], the plaintiff must show the defendant's negligent conduct more probably than not was a cause of the injury."[75] "The defendant's negligence need not be the sole cause of the plaintiff's injury, but simply a cause or a contributing cause."[76] If the defendant's negligence is not a substantial factor in producing the harm, then there is no liability.[77]

For example, a soccer player sprained her left ankle while playing in a home game. She received therapy for the injured ankle and was told that she would have to tape it once she was cleared to return. She attended a game in uniform on January 14, 2003, but did not play. She told her coach that she would not be allowed to play until the physician released her. She once again suited up for a game on January 18, again without taping her ankle or wearing a brace. Although she intended not to play, she did play at the request of the coach for the last five minutes. Three days later, although still not released to play, she suited up for a game. The coach asked her if she was ready to play. The soccer player said that she would "love to play" and asked a teammate to tape her ankle. During the game, she was kicked in the right leg, suffering multiple fractures. She brought suit for her injury because she was allowed to play when she had not been cleared medically because of the injury to her left ankle. The trial court granted the defendant's motion for summary judgment and the defendant appealed.[78]

The court of appeals noted that the plaintiff's testimony supported a finding that she had played "very well" and had "shut down "one of the best people on [the opposing team]."[79] Her injured left ankle evidently had not impeded her mobility or agility. The issue before the court was "[B]ut for the defendant's action in putting [the plaintiff] into a soccer game when she had not been released from her doctor to play soccer, [plaintiff] would not have broken her left leg."[80] The appellate court held that the injury to plaintiff's right leg was not caused by the preexisting injury to her left ankle. She lost.

In another case, the fire bell sounded at Sarah T. Reed High School. The students saw smoke while proceeding to the designated exit. The school administration quickly contained the fire and blocked the students from exiting the building. The students, unaware that the fire was contained, complained of eye irritation and smoke inhalation. The students blocked from leaving feared for their safety. The situation became chaotic. A student, in the melee, was struck on the head and on the knee by a piece of wood and was injured. The student brought suit for her injuries.

The Louisiana Court of Appeals heard the appeal from the Orleans Parish School Board.[81] The district court found for the plaintiff and awarded $175,000 in general damages for bodily injuries, $19,294.35 for medical expenses, and $2,700 for expert fees.[82] The appellate court found that the school district had a duty to protect students from harm. That duty encompassed "maintaining control of emergency situations that could place the students in harm's way."[83] The fire alarm directs students to evacuate the school building to a safe location. It is a procedure practiced regularly in schools across the nation. Once the alarm sounded, placing in motion a known procedure, the school staff was responsible "for allowing [the students] to do so in a safe and orderly manner."[84]

The staff changed the procedure and the students responded by attempting to force their way out of the building that they thought was on fire. In finding causation for the injury, the court wrote, "But for the change in the evacuation procedures, the students probably would not have resorted to forcing their way out of the building. . . . The staff improperly executed the evacuation procedure and these actions were the cause in fact of Ms. Mosley's injuries."[85] The plaintiff student prevailed.

In many regards this case could also be reviewed through the duty owed lens of proper instructions. Under this standard of care, proper instructions had been given but the school staff had not allowed the students to follow those directions by blocking the students from completing the directions.

Even if the defendant's act or omission met the standards of the but-for test and the substantial factor test, the defendant's actions may not be the proximate or legal cause of the plaintiff's injury. The doctrine of proximate cause limits the liability of defendants.

Proximate cause, or legal cause as it has sometimes been called, has been linked to duty in that a reasonable person has a duty to protect an individual from foreseeable harm. The conduct of an actor creates a zone of danger. Individuals within that zone of danger become foreseeable plaintiffs. If it is foreseeable that a particular action, or omission to act, can cause harm to a specific individual, then proximate cause is established. Therefore, the link between proximate cause and duty is that a duty is only owed to individuals who are foreseeably within the zone of apparent danger created by the act.[86] For example, if a student strikes another student with a fist and the school officials had no knowledge of the student's propensity to commit violent acts, the attack is not foreseeable.[87] Obviously, once it is known that a particular student has a propensity to act in a dangerous manner, that knowledge serves as foreseeability, thus requiring a standard of care regarding that particular student.

For example, Ms. Smith (see "Ms. Smith's Very Bad Day" in chapter 3) knew that Steve had a propensity to either not wear his goggles or take them off. Therefore, it is foreseeable that Steve would not wear his goggles for the experiment in which he was injured. Does this make Steve a foreseeable plaintiff?

Conversely, even though the defendant school district knew that particular students occasionally played on the roof, "stepping on a skylight is an extraordinary occurrence which need not be guarded against."[88] Similarly, a New York Appellate Court found that the injury caused to a student sitting on the hood of a car talking to his friends in the car when a student unexpectedly put the car in motion was not foreseeable and thus was not the proximate cause of the injury.[89]

The reasonable person test of duty owed and the foreseeability standard of proximate cause are closely related. Public schools owe a duty to use ordinary care and to take reasonable steps to minimize foreseeable risks to students,[90] thereby providing a safe school environment. An example of the fit between cause-in-fact and the proximate cause foreseeability element is found in *Cedar Falls v. Cedar Falls School District*.[91] In September 1995, the city of Cedar Falls held its annual safety program for kindergarten students. During the program several of the students went over to an unattended golf cart with the key in the ignition. One of the students apparently stepped on the accelerator, releasing the brake. The cart surged forward, pinning a kindergarten student against the side of an ambulance. The student later died from his injuries. Applying the cause-in-fact analysis, the court asserted that a jury could find that the accident would not have occurred "but for" the negligence in supervising the students. "The cart would not have started had the children been prevented from playing on it."[92] Furthermore, the court applied the proximate cause analysis to the facts and concluded, "Because it was foreseeable the children would be curious and interested in the golf cart, the jury could conclude their conduct fell within the original risk created by the District's actions."[93]

SUFFICIENT INJURY

Injury is not presumed; the plaintiff must show actual injury or harm. In cases where an injury has occurred due to the negligence of another, the plaintiff has a duty to mitigate his or her damages. For example, a student who meets the first three elements of the tort of negligence but only sustains an abrasion that heals quickly may not meet this test. The sufficiency of the injury is often not reported because if the injury was slight the case may have been settled out of court or a motion to dismiss may have been granted. Most discussions of injury involve the severity of the injury. If negligence is proved, then the severity of the injury is used to calculate the monetary award.[94]

However, in a Pennsylvania case a student was injured when he walked between two parked school buses and was struck by an employee of the Ridley School District driving a vehicle owned by the school district. Under Pennsylvania law, a plaintiff may only recover for a negligent act during the operation of a local agency's (school

WHEN AN ACCIDENT HAPPENS—WHAT NEXT?

Christian M. Keiner, J.D.

Even the most careful principal can face a major accident to a student occurring either on campus or during off-campus school-sanctioned events such as field trips or athletic contests. Hopefully, the school has adopted a school safety plan that guides a principal's responses (see chapter 18, "Safety Plans, Communication, and the Press"). In the most straightforward circumstance, a single student has an accident on campus that causes bodily injury. In more complex circumstances, multiple students are injured off campus in, for example, a bus accident. In the most difficult circumstance, multiple students are injured on or off campus in a highly visible catastrophic event, such as a natural disaster or amusement park ride breakdown during a sanctioned graduation trip.

In the case of the single student, the principal should immediately check the emergency information in the student's file. The parent(s) should be promptly informed. The parents or school should have the student treated as soon as possible by the student's own doctor, or, if necessary, transported to the emergency room. Depending upon local or state law, there may be restrictions upon the student receiving medical treatment absent parental consent. Follow the emergency information and parental directives whenever possible, unless the situation is life threatening. If the principal takes any written statements from student or adult witnesses to the accident, the principal should assume any written material will be discoverable during subsequent litigation. Depending upon local school district policies, the principal may or may not be tasked with this fact-gathering duty. In a major on- or off-campus accident involving multiple students, the injuries will likely require emergency attention from the fire department or EMTs. The principal will be involved quite quickly in rumor control, with both parents and media. The principal should follow the same steps above, with notification as quickly as possible to parents of those students suffering injury. However, in catastrophic circumstances, the emergency response team(s) will be making decisions regarding emergency treatment.

The principal may, again depending upon local custom or school safety policy, notify all parents of the circumstances by telephonic or written communication to reassure the parents of noninvolved students. Again depending upon state law or local custom, the principal may also have to enforce restrictions upon the media entering campus for pictures or live "minicam" television news reports. Typically, media does not have access to students for comments or photographs without parental permission. The principal must be aware that any on-camera remarks the principal makes "in the heat of the moment" will be preserved for some time. If the school district is large enough to have a designated media spokesperson, let that spokesperson attend to the media.

The principal in these more difficult circumstances is like a good city mayor—making sure the needs of those injured are attended to, reassuring those who are not injured, and ensuring everyone clears the campus (or off-campus event) safely and without additional injuries caused by panic.

district) vehicle. In order for this provision to be used to overcome governmental immunity, the injury must involve a permanent loss of a bodily function or result in a permanent disfigurement. The student sustained compound facture of his right arm. The injury left a small mark or scar. The jury found that the four-millimeter mark did not constitute disfigurement, thus the plaintiff was denied damages for pain and suffering.[95] In this case the injury was not sufficient to meet the standard specified in the Pennsylvania law.

NOTES

1. W. Page Keeton, *Prosser and Keeton on Torts*, 2 (5th ed. 1984). ("The metaphor is apparent: a tort is a conduct which is twisted, or crooked, not straight.")

2. *Id.*

3. For example, in a criminal trial, the burden carried by the state is to prove the allegations beyond a reasonable doubt. In a civil trial for tort liability, the plaintiff must prove the more relaxed standard of preponderance of the evidence.

4. William D. Valente with C. M. Valente, *The Law in the Schools* (4th ed. 1998).

5. "'Intent' is the word commonly used to describe the purposes to bring about *stated physical consequences;* the more remote objective which inspires the act and the intent is called 'motive'" (Keeton, *supra* note 1 at 35, italics in original). It is a volitional act as opposed to a negligent act. The most common intentional torts are assault, battery, false imprisonment, infliction of mental distress, trespass to land or chattel, and conversion. "Negligence differs from an intentional tort in that negligent acts are neither expected nor intended, whereas an intentional tort can be both anticipated and intended" (Kern Alexander and M. David Alexander, *American Public School Law*, 555 (5th ed. 2001)).

6. Strict liability occurs when an injury results from the creation of an unusual hazard, such as the storage and transportation of explosives or the possession of large, dangerous animals. It is liability without fault. A trampoline was not held to be an abnormally dangerous instrumentality, thus a school district was not held strictly liable for the severe injury to a sixth-grade student who used it (Fallon v. Indian Trail School, 500 N.E.2d 101 (Ill.App. Ct. 1986)). For a discussion of strict liability as applied to the sexual abuse of students, *see*, Todd A. DeMitchell and Richard Fossey, "Strict Liability Under Title IX for Employee Sexual Abuse of Students: Leija v. Canutillo Independent School District," *International Journal of Educational Reform*, 107–114 (1996).

7. 42 U.S.C. § 1983 (1994). "Under section 1983, the plaintiff must show that the school district established a policy, practice, or custom of reckless indifference to the plaintiff's rights." David J. Sperry, Philip T. K. Daniel, Dixie Snow Huefner, and E. Gordon Gee, *Education Law and the Public Schools: A Compendium*, 1090 (2nd ed. 1998).

8. *Id.* at 1068.

9. Keeton, *supra* note 1.

10. Sperry et al., *supra* note 7.

11. Jonathan A. v. Board of Education of the City of New York, 779 N.Y.S.2d 3, 6 (A.D. 1 Dept. 2004).

12. *Restatement (Second) of Torts* § 320 comment b at 131.

13. Mirand v. City of New York, 614 N.Y.S.2d 372, 375 (Ct.App. 1994).

14. Vernonia School District 47J v. Acton, 115 S.Ct. 2386 (1995). For a discussion of in loco parentis, *see*, Todd A. DeMitchell, "The Duty to Protect: Blackstone's Doctrine of *In Loco Parentis*: A Lens for Viewing the Sexual Abuse of Students," *Brigham Young University Journal of Education and Law* 17 (2002).

15. Collette v. Tolleson Unified School District, No. 214, 54 P.3d 828, 835 (Ariz.App. Div. 1 2002).

16. 115 P.3d 342, 346 (Wash.App. Div. 3 2005).

17. Diaz v. Krob, 636 N.E.2d 1231 (Ill.App.3 Dist. 1994).

18. Rock v. State, 681 A.2d 901 (R.I. 1996).

19. Bellman v. San Francisco High School District, (1938) 11 Cal.2d 576, 582.

20. Marquay v. Eno, 662 A.2d 272 (N.H. 1995).

21. Levandoski v. Jackson County Sch. Dist., 328 So.2d 339, 342 (Miss. 1976).

22. Dunn v. Unified School District No. 367, 40 P.3d 315, 326 (Kan.App. 2002).

23. Mirand v. City of New York, 614 N.Y.S.2d 372, 375 (Ct.App. 1994).

24. Wyke v. Polk County School Board, 129 F.3d 560 (11th Cir. 1997).

25. Santanna v. City of New York, 722 N.Y.S.2d 545, 555 (A.D. 1 Dept. 2001).

26. Gonzalez v. City of New York, 730 N.Y.S.2d 154 (A.D. 2 Dept. 2001).

27. Rhea v. Grandview School District, 694 P.2d 666 (Wash. Ct. App. 1985).

28. Hurlburt v. Noxon, 565 N.Y.S.2d 683 (N.Y. Sup. Ct.1990).

29. C.M. v. City of New York, 800 N.Y.S.2d 898, 900 (Sup. 2005).

30. *Id.* Even though the sexual assault would not have occurred absent the employee's power over the student by virtue of his employment, the school was not found to be vicariously liable for the injury. The court also found that the school district had not negligently supervised the teacher because it did not have notice of inappropriate behavior.

31. *See*, Summers v. St. Andrew's Episcopal School, 759 So.2d 1203 (Miss. 2000); Coleman v. Joyner, 593 So. 2d 451 (1992); and Hernandez v. Christopher Robin Academy, 714 N.Y.S.2d 518 (N.Y.App. Div. 2000). Dunn v. Unified School District No. 367, 40 P.3d 315, 328 (Kan.App. 2002). (There is no question that a school has a duty to provide a suitable environment conducive to the general health, safety, and welfare of each student. Even though a school has such a duty, it cannot be an insurer against all accidents.)

32. Brownell v. Los Angeles Unified School District, 5 Cal. Rptr 2d 756 (Cal. Ct.App. 1992).

33. This is generally true unless the school assumes a responsibility that the students have come to rely upon for their safety. A good example of expanding the duty owed is that the school handbook states that supervision begins at 8:00, but the administration starts supervising students at 7:30 (when the first students arrive). If students and parents have come to rely upon that additional supervision because the school has undertaken to provide it, the school must discharge that duty in a reasonable manner. *See*, Johnson v. Ouachita Parish Police Jury, 377 So.2d 397 (La. Ct.App. 1979), in which it was held that a school district was under no legal duty to provide a school safety patrol, but once it assumed the duty it must act reasonably to meet the duty.

34. Summers v. Cambridge Joint School District No. 432, 88 P.3d 772 (Idaho 2004).

35. Nelda H. Cambron-McCabe, Martha M. McCarthy, and Stephen B. Thomas, *Public School Law: Teachers' and Students' Rights*, 469 (5th ed. 2004).

36. In a nationwide study by LRP, negligent supervision accounted for 43 percent of the school negligence suits resulting in awards. Rachael Kaiman (Ed.), *School Negligence and Safety Claims: An Inside Look at Limiting Your School's Exposure*, 3 (2003).

37. Karen-Ann Broe and Nancy W. Brown (2004), *Preventing Catastrophic Student Injuries*. Paper Presentation, Education Law Association, Tucson, AZ at 19.

38. Michael Imber and Tyll van Gell, *Education Law*, 458 (2nd ed. 2000).

39. Vonungren v. Morris Central School District, 658 N.Y.S.2d 760, 761 (A.D.3 Dept. 1997).

40. Shin v. Sunriver Prep. Sch. Inc., 111 P.3d 762 (Or. App. 2005).

41. 150 N.W.2d 460 (1967).

42. National Center for Education Statistics, *Indicators of School Crime and Safety: 2005*, Indicator 12: Bullying at School. Site accessed 12/26/05, http://nces.ed.gov/programs/crimeindicators/indicators.asp?pubpage number=12.

43. Cori Brewster and Jennifer Railsback (2003), *Schoolwide Prevention of Bullying*, Northwest Regional Educational Laboratory. Site visited 12/29/05, http://www.nwrel.org/request/dec01/bullying.pdf at 7. According to the authors, "10 percent of students who drop out of school do so because of repeated bullying; bullies identified by age eight are six times more likely to be convicted of a crime by age 24 and five times more likely than non-bullies to end up with serious criminal records by the age of 30," at 6 (internal citations omitted).

44. It should be noted that the statistics gathered for the report do not include student experiences with bullying at school below grade six.

45. *Bullying and Harassment in American K-12 Public Schools: Are Schools and Courts Working Together*, Education Law Association Conference, Memphis, TN, November 2005 at 3.

46. For example, *see*, New Hampshire RSA 193-F et seq.

47. Fred Hartmeister, *Preventing Bullying: At the Intersection Between Legislation, Litigation, Research, and Reality*, Education Law Association Conference, Memphis, TN, November 2005 at 3.

48. *See*, McAdams v. Board of Education of Rocky Point Union Free School District, 216 F. Supp.2d 86 (E.D.N.Y. 2002).

49. Marquay v. Eno, 662 A.2d 272, 280 (N.H. 1995).

50. Bush v. Oscada Area Schools, 250 N.W.2d 759 (1977).

51. Baker v. Briarcliff School District, 613 N.Y.S.2d 660 (A.D. 2 Dept. 1994).

52. LaValley v. Stanford, 70 N.Y.S. 249 (1947).

53. Fred Hartmeister, *Surviving as a Teacher: The Legal Dimension*, 187 (1995).

54. Lottie v. Edwards-Knox Central School District, 652 N.Y.S.2d 144, 145 (A.D. 3 Dept. 1997).

55. Johnson v. Orleans Parish School Board, 261 So.2d 699 (1972).

56. Keaton v. Hancock County Board of Education, 119 S.W.3d 218, 220 (Tenn. Ct.App. 2003).

57. Cioffi v. Board of Education of City of New York, 278 N.Y.S.2d 249 (N.Y.App.Div. 1967), cited in Charles J. Russo, *Reutter's the Law of Public Education*, 416 (5th ed. 2004).

58. Keeton, *supra* note 1, at 175. "A reasonable person uses the care that a 'reasonably prudent' and 'careful' individual uses in ordinary life to avoid harm or injury to others when faced with certain phenomena and circumstances." Charles J. Russo and Ralph D. Mawdsley, *Education Law*, 6–32 (2004).

59. Cambron-McCabe, *supra* note 35.

60. Benitez v. New York City Board of Education, 543 N.Y.S.2d 29 (N.Y. 1989).

61. Martha M. McCarthy, Nelda H. Cambron-McCabe, and Stephen B. Thomas, *Legal Rights of Teachers and Students*, 26 (2004).

62. Lafayette Parish School Board v. Cormier, 901 So.2d 1197, 1203 (La.App. 3 Cir. 2005). The school district was seeking damages to cover the amount it had paid and would likely pay for the employee's injury through worker's compensation.

63. Moody v. New York City Board of Education, 780 N.Y.S.2d 603, 604 (A.D. 2 Dept. 2004).

64. Janukajtis v. Fallon, 726 N.Y.S.2d 451 (A.D. 2 Dept. 2001). Also *see*, Siegell v. Herricks Union Free School District, 777 N.Y.S2d 148 (A. D. 2 Dept. 2004), in which a student was shoved during a relay race. The court held that the offending student's history of disciplinary problems involving violence was insufficient to place the school on notice that he would injure someone. Absent that type of knowledge, the school district did not have a duty to prevent spontaneous and unforeseeable acts of students.

65. *Id.*

66. 717 N.Y.S.2d 341, 342 (A.D. 2 Dept. 2000).

67. Yurkovich v. Rose, 847 P.2d 925 (Wash. Ct.App. 1993).

68. Brown v. Tesack, 566 So.2d 955, 956 (La. 1990). ("Putting children and flammable mixtures together, unfortunately, more often than not, produces combustion.") at 958.

69. 159 Eng. Rep. 299 (1863).

70. A.C. Ex Real Cooper v. Bellingham School, 105 P.3d 400, 403 (Wash.App.Div. 1 2004).

71. Douglas v. Board of Education, 468 N.E.2d 473 (1984).

72. Roman v. Board of Education of the City of New York, 780 N.Y.S.D.2d 5 (N.Y.App. Div. 2004).

73. Alexander and Alexander, *supra* note 5, at 558.

74. Keeton, *supra* note 1, at 265.

75. Nisbet v. Bucher, 949 S.W.2d 111, 115 (Mo.App. E.D. 1997).

76. *Id.*

77. For example, a failure of the plaintiff to prove causation was the "second most common successful defense" in liability cases for student suicide (Perry A. Zirkel and Richard Fossey, "Liability for Student Suicide," 197 *Education Law Reporter* 489, 493 (2005)).

78. Stephenson v. Commercial Travelers Ins., 893 So.2d 180 (La.App. 3 Cir. 2005).

79. *Id.* at 185.

80. *Id.* at 183.

81. Mosley v. Orleans Parish School Board, 898 So.2d 524 (La.App. 4 Cir. 2005).

82. *Id.* at 525.

83. *Id.* at 527.

84. *Id.*

85. *Id.* at 528.

86. *See*, Palsgraf v. Long Island Railroad Company, 162 N.E. 99 (N.Y. 1928). In this case, two men ran for a train that was departing the railway platform. One successfully jumped on the train. The second jumped but appeared to be ready to fall from the moving train. One guard on the train tried to pull him onto the train and another on the platform pushed him from behind. The pushing and pulling dislodged a package, which fell to the tracks and exploded. He was carrying fireworks. The explosion caused the overhead sign to fall on Helen Palsgraf, who was many feet away from the action. Mrs. Palsgraf brought suit against the railway company. Was Mrs. Palsgraf a foreseeable plaintiff? The court said no.

87. Emery v. Chapman, 495 So.2d 371 (La.App. 3 Cir. 1986).

88. Clifford v. Sachem Central School District, 707 N.Y.S.2d 133, 134 (A.D. 2 Dept. 2000).

89. Organ v. Yorktown Central Sch. Dist., 703 N.Y.S. 2d (N.Y.A.D. 2 2000).

90. L.W. v. McComb Separate Mun. Sch. Dist., 754 So.2d 1136, 1143 (Miss. 1999).

91. 617 N.W.2d 11 (Iowa 2000).

92. *Id.* at 17.

93. *Id.* at 18.

94. Most awards are compensatory, in which the court fashions a remedy, usually in the form of money, calculated to make the person "whole." When the court believes that the defendant's actions are egregious, the court may levy a punitive damage award as a signal dissuading others of following the pattern of behavior.

95. Alexander v. Benson, 812 A.2d 785 (Pa. Comwlth. 2002).

5

Defenses to a Finding of Negligence: When an Accident Happens—What Next?

Christian Keiner, J.D.

Once the plaintiff has established the prima facie case of negligence by proving duty owed, breach, causation, and sufficient injury, the defendant has the opportunity to assert a defense. There are several defenses available to defendants to rebut charges of negligence.

ACCIDENTS/ACTS OF GOD

First, not all bad things that happen to individuals are a result of someone's negligence. Accidents do happen, although in our litigious society whenever an injury occurs there is a vigorous search to find someone liable. The simple truth is that sometimes accidents do happen and no amount of reasonable action on the part of another could prevent them. Often, when this defense is asserted the act that gave rise to the injury is ascribed as an act of God, something unforeseen and outside of the control of the participants.

IMMUNITY

A second defense is sovereign immunity, or governmental immunity. This defense has deep roots in common law where the "king could do no wrong" and could only be sued if the king agreed to being sued.

This concept of immunity was transplanted to government. In 1788, a wagon owner sued the Men of Devon County, who were responsible for maintaining roads. The wagon owner's wagon broke down as a result of a bridge being in disrepair. The court stated that it was better for an individual to sustain an injury than the public an inconvenience.[1] This case formed the basis for sovereign immunity for government until *Molitor v. Kaneland*.[2] In this case, the Supreme Court of Illinois ruled in favor of the plaintiff, who was injured after getting off a school bus. The court asserted that sovereign immunity was no longer tenable because it rested on a "rotten foundation."

Since *Molitor*, immunity has been available but only within limits established by individual state law. The type and extent of immunity enjoyed by school districts as governmental entities vary from state to state. For example, Illinois provides immunity for the exercise of discretion of some state actors.[3] In Mississippi, educators are immune from liability if and only if they used ordinary care in controlling and disciplining students.[4] In South Carolina, a governmental entity is not liable for a loss resulting from the "responsibility or duty including but not limited to supervision, protection, control, confinement, or custody of any student . . . except when the responsibility or duty is exercised in a grossly negligent manner."[5] Furthermore, a California case[6] upheld an immunity statute for field trips. If the case study "A Field Trip to the Seashore" (see chapter 3) took place in California the educators may not be liable because of immunity. It would not mean that they did not act negligently, only that they are immune for their negligent acts.

ASSUMPTION OF THE RISK

The third defense is assumption of the risk. Generally, this defense asserts that an individual who voluntarily assumes the risk of an activity cannot recover for injuries associated with that activity. It assumes that he or she knew of and appreciated the risks associated with that activity and still volunteered to participate. In effect, an assumption of risk transfers the foreseeability of harm to the plaintiff.[7] The most common application of assumption of the risk is found when attending ball games. A spectator assumes the risk normally associated with attending a ball game and therefore cannot sue a batter who hits a foul ball that strikes and injures the spectator.

In school settings, assumption of risk is most often associated with extracurricular sports.[8] "Participants are held to assume normal risks by their actual or implied consents to play the game."[9] For example, a student's ankle was fractured sliding into a base. The coach was not liable for the injury because such a risk is an inherent part of the game, and the risk was known to the plaintiff and assumed by the plaintiff.[10] In another case, a high school custodian allowed a number of high school students to play basketball in the school's gymnasium during the semester break. During the game two students collided when scrambling for a rebound. One of the students suffered a fractured spine. A lawsuit for negligence was brought against the school district. The Idaho Supreme Court held that the student plaintiff had assumed the risk of normal physical contact associated with playing basketball. In addition, the court found that the absence of supervision was not the proximate cause of the injury. The court asserted that had a coach or teacher been supervising the game, the collision and resulting injury would not have been prevented. The student lost.[11]

Another losing case for the student plaintiff involved a member of the seventh grade volleyball team. The athlete was struck in the back of the head during a volleyball practice. While there was some dispute as to whether the injury occurred after the coach signaled the end of the practice or during the practice, the court upheld the grant of summary judgment dismissing the negligent supervision claim. The court held, "Players who voluntarily join in extracurricular interscholastic sports assume the risks to which their roles expose them but not risks which are 'unreasonably increased or concealed.'"[12] The risks associated with playing volleyball were not unreasonably increased when the student athlete walked off the court, whether play was ended or not.

The key to assumption of the risk is the knowing assumption of the risk. For example, a young student who does not understand the danger of an act typically is not considered to have assumed the risk of the act. The typical test for this defense for children is whether a particular child, considering her or his age, background, and inherent intelligence, indulges in the gross disregard of his or her own safety in the face of known, understood, and perceived danger.[13]

On a related matter, generally, a signed permission slip to attend a field trip does not mean a student has assumed a risk, nor does it amount to a waiver of liability. For example, a state court found that "[m]inors can waive nothing. In the law they are helpless, so much that their representatives can waive nothing for them."[14] Permission slips at their best inform parents and guardians that their child will be away from the campus. It is good public relations but a poor defense for the negligent behavior of an educator. Educators should not base their behavior on a permission slip. Prudent educators assume that they have no immunity and act as if their decisions can result in injury and liability.

CONTRIBUTORY NEGLIGENCE

The fourth defense is contributory negligence. Contributory negligence occurs when the plaintiff's actions or omissions are negligent and contribute to his or her own injury by falling below the standard expected for his or her own protection. "However, since a child is not expected to act with the same standard of care as an adult, teachers have more difficulty in showing contributory negligence than they would if the plaintiff was an adult."[15] The actions of the student plaintiff must be reasonable for a child of similar age, maturity, intelligence, and experience. Students are usually not considered to be contributorily negligent unless they understood and appreciated the danger posed by the activity. For example, a six-year-old child ran into the street and the side of a car while returning to school. Because of his age, the court found that the six-year-old did "not share in the fault for his injury because he acted in a manner that could have been expected of a child of his age."[16] But, a high school senior who was an accomplished diver and swimmer was solely responsible for her injuries when she attempted to execute a shallow dive.[17]

In another case, a middle school assistant principal attended a basketball tournament held at the local high school to watch his twelve-year-old son play. There were three sets of bleachers set up for the three basketball games. The father changed bleachers each time his son changed courts. At the third bleacher he took a seat on the highest row, leaned back after sitting there for ten minutes, crossed his leg, and fell to the floor. The third set of bleachers did not have a back support. He sued the school district for the injuries that he sustained in the fall. The trial court found that the father was contributorily negligent and that his conduct proximately caused the injury. On appeal, the Court of Appeals of Indiana remanded the case to decide whether the plaintiff knew or should have known that there was no back behind the last tier of seats. At the trial the plaintiff stated that he did not think about whether he was seated on the final row.[18] Judge Baker dissented, arguing that the plaintiff "may not have known that the bleachers did not have a back support is of no moment, inasmuch as any reasonably prudent person would have checked before leaning backwards."[19]

In the case study "A Field Trip to the Seashore" (see chapter 3), could the school raise the defense that the two students who drowned contributed to their deaths by wandering away and not staying close? How could the plaintiff counter this assertion? Similarly, the defense of contributory negligence can be raised in the "Ms. Smith's Very Bad Day" scenario. While Ms. Smith did not instruct the students to wear their goggles, should Steve have worn his goggles because he was working with caustic chemicals, had received previous instruction about wearing goggles when working with these chemicals, and the textbook he was instructed to read prior to the experiment contained an explicit warning regarding wearing goggles?

COMPARATIVE NEGLIGENCE

In traditional contributory negligence cases, once the defense has been established the plaintiff is barred from any recover. However, in many states contributory negligence and assumption of the risk have been replaced or modified with comparative negligence. Comparative negligence apportions liability; thus it is less harsh than the all-or-nothing aspect of contributory negligence. Comparative negligence assesses the degree of plaintiff's fault on a percentage basis. For example, a student was injured while using a band saw. The student did not follow the directions regarding not removing the blade guard, and the teacher only observed the student once during a half-hour session. The other students were using handsaws instead of the power saw. The jury found that the teacher acted negligently and returned a judgment for $100,000. The teacher raised a defense of comparative negligence, arguing that the student was contributorily negligent. Using comparative negligence, the jury found the teacher 60 percent negligent and the student 40 percent contributorily negligent. Thus, the student received compensation in the amount of $60,000.

A jury in Kansas found a school district 90 percent negligent and two students at fault for 10 percent of their injuries. The two high school students walked rapidly towards a closed hallway door at their high school. The two boys reached the door at the same time and reached for the crossbar to open the door. One of the student's hands slipped, shattering the plate glass in the door. The glass was not safety glass and it shattered severely, injuring the two students.[20]

In *Brown v. Tesack* (the duplicating fluid case in which a student was burned, discussed in chapter 4), the jury originally awarded $451,219.13, to be paid by the two defendants, with 90 percent of the fault apportioned to one defendant and 10 percent to the other defendant.[21] But on appeal, the school district was assessed to be 55 percent at fault, the first defendant 35 percent at fault, and the other defendant 10 percent at fault.[22]

"LET THE MASTER ANSWER"

If a teacher is sued for negligence and he or she is found negligent and the defenses discussed above result in a monetary judgment against the teacher, must the teacher pay the damages awarded to the plaintiff? Typically the answer is no. A settled principle of common law holds the master liable for acts of a servant if the servant is acting within the scope of the servant's employment. This master-servant relationship of the master answering for the deeds of the servant is called *respondeat superior*, or "let the master answer."[23] The key to *respondeat superior* is the requirement that the servant is acting within the scope of his or her employment. Intentional acts such as assault or battery causing injury typically do not invoke the protection of *respondeat superior* because the employer typically does not hire an employee to assault or batter others. In the situation discussed above, the district as the master would pay the $60,000 judgment against the wood shop teacher, or servant. However, it must be noted that a teacher may lose the protection of *respondeat superior* if he or she willfully and persistently disregards lawful directives.

For example, in the "Recess Duty at the Swings" scenario in chapter 3, Mr. Roberts could possibly lose the monetary protection if he had persistently and willfully refused to go out to his duty. This happens rarely, but it can happen. An employee's willful and persistent failure to follow the legitimate and reasonable direction of the supervisor places the employee in jeopardy of being charged with insubordination and also of losing the protection of *respondeat superior* if an injury occurs.

In the vast majority of cases a teacher and/or a principal who is sued for negligence and loses is held harmless for monetary damages. But that does not mean that the educator does not suffer harm. Knowing that our action or failure to act caused an injury can be a heavy burden to bear. It is best not to rely on the defenses or the protection of *respondeat superior.* A strong offense in which the educator, led by the principal, develops habits of action, which include reasonable responses to foreseeable injuries, is the better game plan.

NOTES

1. Russell v. Men of Devon, 100 Eng. Rep. 359.
2. 163 N.E.2d 89 (1959).
3. 745 ILCS 10/1-101 et seq. (West 1994).
4. Mississippi Tort Claims Act, Miss. Code Ann. § 11-46-1 et seq. (Supp. 1999). Also *see,* R.C. 2744.03(A)(5) and (6), which provides immunity for Ohio educators, and V.C.T.A. Education Code § 22.051(a), which provides immunity from personal liability in Texas. In Minnesota only discretionary acts and not ministerial acts are granted immunity (Minn. Stat. § 466.03, subd. 6 (2002)). *See,* Anderson v. Anoka Hennepin School District 11, 655 N.W.2d 847 (Minn.App. 2003), in which a wood shop teacher's directions regarding when to use a blade guard on a power saw were considered ministerial. While the court did not decide if the teacher acted negligently in not instructing the student to use the blade guard, the court held that the classroom directions did not constitute discretion.
5. S.C. Code Ann. § 15-78-60(25) (Supp. 1999).
6. Casterson v. Superior Court, 123 Cal.Rptr.2d 637 (Cal.App. 6 Dist. 2002), citing West's Ann. Cal. Educ. Code § 35330. This case found that Section 35330 applied to the acts of employees acting within the scope of their employment as well as to school districts specifically mentioned in the statute.
7. David J. Sperry, Philip T. K. Daniel, Dixie Snow Huefner, and E. Gordon Gee, *Education Law and the Public Schools: A Compendium* (2nd ed. 1998).
8. *See,* Kahn v. East Side Union High School District, 75 P.3d 30 (2003), in which a swimmer broke her neck while practicing a racing dive. In order to overcome the assumption of risk defense the activity would have to be totally outside of the range of activities ordinarily associated with the sport; Serrell v. Connetquot Central School District, 798 N.Y.S2d 493, 494 (A.D. 2 Dept. 2005). ("The injured plaintiff, an experienced high school football player, voluntarily assumed the risk of injury by participating in the varsity football practice in which he was injured.")

9. Kern Alexander and M. David Alexander, *American Public School Law*, 578 (5th ed. 2001).

10. Kelly v. McCarrick, 841 A.2d 869 (Md. Spec. App. 2004).

11. Albers v. Independent School District #302 of Lewis City, 487 P.2d 936 (1971).

12. Hochreiter v. Diocese of Buffalo, 764 N.Y.S.2d 753, 754 (A.D. 4 Dept. 2003).

13. Simmons v. Beauregard Parish School Board, 315 So. 2d 883 (1975).

14. Khoury v. Saik, 33 So.2d 616, 617 (1948).

15. Alexander and Alexander, *supra* note 9, at 570.

16. Sutton v. Duplessis, 584 So.2d 362 (La.Ct.App. 1991), cited in Charles J. Russo, *Reutter's The Law of Public Education*, 425 (5th ed. 2004).

17. Aronson v. Horace Mann-Barnard School, 637 N.Y.S.2d 410 (App.Div. 1996).

18. Funston v. School Town of Munster, 822 N.E.2d 985 (Ind.App. 2005).

19. *Id.* at 989.

20. Dunn v. Unified School District No. 367, 40 P.3d 315 (Kan.App. 2002).

21. Brown v. Tesack, 566 So.2d 955, 956 (La. 1990).

22. *Id.* at 958.

23. For a discussion of *respondeat superior* as it applies to sexual abuse of students perpetrated by school employees, *see*, Richard Fossey and Todd A. DeMitchell, "'Let the Master Answer': Holding Schools Vicariously Liable When Employees Sexually Abuse Children," *Journal of Law & Education* 575 (1996).

IV

APPLICATIONS OF TORT LIABILITY

6

Hazing: More Than an Innocent Injury

The discussion thus far provides a framework from which principals can analyze situations and make reasonable decisions to reduce the foreseeability of injury. These elements have broad applicability. This chapter and the following chapters apply the principles of tort liability to specific school contexts that principals all too often face.

The first situation raises the question: to what extent does a school owe a duty to its students who are injured away from school while taking part in a hazing ritual of an on-campus club or activity?

Hazing is not harmless pranks as parts of the rites of passage. Hazing is more than silly actions that are merely momentarily embarrassing. Hazing is more than good-natured fun for all participants. Hazing involves abuse often linked to humiliation. "Hazing refers to any activity expected of someone joining a group (or to maintain full status in a group) that humiliates, degrades or risks emotional and/or physical harm, regardless of the person's willingness to participate."[1]

> A 12-year-old seventh grade student in Michigan spent four days in the hospital for blood loss, a broken leg, and other injuries after older students attacked him during football practice in a team ritual known as eighth-grade-hit-day. (Karen-Ann Broe, Esq., Senior Risk Analyst, United Educators)[2]

The May 2003 "powder puff" touch football incident may well serve as the poster for high school hazing. The videotape, which aired on the national news networks, portrayed the descent from harmless razzing to injury and degradation. In this case, five girls went to the hospital after being punched and slapped as well as having paint, feces, and trash dumped on them. Thirty-one students were suspended.[3]

The resulting court case focused on whether school authorities had the authority to impose discipline for acts that took place away from school and were not school sanctioned or school sponsored.[4] The court found that the school had the authority based in part on a school policy that prohibits hazing. While the issue in this case was not one of school negligence, it is, however, instructive. Had the court found that the school had no authority over the students, it is likely that the school would then owe no duty to the students.[5] If a duty is owed, then the school authorities must act reasonably to avoid foreseeable injuries. Arguably, the anti-hazing policy is directed at protecting students as well as preserving order. Could the injured students in this situation have sued the school district based on the fact that it prohibited hazing and took disciplinary action against those who hazed? It is possible that the injured students were owed a duty as identified by the school handbook. If a duty was owed, did the school foresee the possibility of harm arising from the off-campus powder puff touch football game and did they act reasonably in light of this foreseeability?

An example of potential school district liability for hazing injuries is found in the state of Washington, where its Supreme Court held that a school district could be held liable. The Franklin Pierce School District knew of ongoing hazing by one of its school clubs. James Chappel, an initiate into the club, fell and broke his ankle while blindfolded at an off-campus initiation. He was made to believe that he was jumping into a pool and instead dropped three feet down an incline. A faculty advisor had helped plan the "leap trick" as well as the "swat line" but did not supervise the event. The court found that the school had exerted supervisory control over the club, including its initiations.[6] Therefore, the school district could be held liable for the off-campus injury. Clearly, the potential liability of schools and their personnel increases if liability can extend, at least in specific situations, beyond the schoolhouse gate.

Weddle, in an analysis of hazing and negligent supervision, advises, "What is 'manifest' to a court should be equally obvious to a school:

simply sending the hazing off campus is no real solution."[7] Turning a blind eye to hazing is not the answer. In addition to the legal duty owed to students, is there not a professional duty that recognizes that hazing often involves the strong asserting their power over the weak? The initiate to a club often does not have the power to resist those who hold the power to admit or not to admit. While as adults, we may say they can walk away or just say no, I am not so sure that most teenagers possess that type of strength. Joining and being part of a group is important to adolescents. Is it not our professional responsibility as well as our legal duty to provide an environment in which students do not have to suffer degrading, humiliating, or harmful acts just for the privilege of being allowed to join other students?[8]

NOTES

1. "Hazing Defined." Site visited 8/25/05, www.stophazing.org/definition .html at 1.
2. Karen-Ann Broe (November 2004), *Preventing Catastrophic Student Injuries.* Paper Presentation, Education Law Association, Tucson, AZ at 23.
3. Nelda Cambron-McCabe and Ellen V. Bueschel, "Where Does Tradition End and Hazing Begin? Implications for School District Policy," 196 *Education Law Reporter* 19 (2005).
4. Gendelman v. Glenbrook North High School, 2003 WL 21209880, No. 3 C 3288 N.D. (Ill. May 23, 2003).
5. *Id.* at 5. The judge wrote, "When one set of students sets to prey upon another set of students in a ritualistic exercise, the consequences of which will necessarily affect students' relationships while they are in attendance at the same school, the ability of school officials to act in the area and discipline those who went beyond the pale of tolerable student behavior is manifest."
6. Chappel v. Franklin Pierce School District, No. 402, 426 P.2d 471 (Wash. 1967).
7. Daniel B. Weddle, "Dangerous Games: Student Hazing and Negligent Supervision," *ELA Notes,* 2005 (40) 3–9.
8. Cambron-McCabe and Bueschel, as well as Weddle, *supra,* offer excellent recommendations for developing hazing policies. *See* also, http://stophazing .org and http://hazing.hanknuwer.com for more information on hazing.

7

Negligent Hiring: Did We Hire the Wrong Person?

The next issue concerns the liability of school districts for hiring an employee who later injures a third party/student. Can schools be held liable if their hiring process is negligent?[1]

This situation involves the tort of negligent hiring. I first learned about negligent hiring when I was the director of Personnel and Labor Relations for a California school district. I was working at my desk when my assistant brought an unknown individual to my open door. The individual reached out with an envelope in his hand and said those words that can chill an educator's heart—"You are served." With a slight smile, he made a notation on his notebook, turned on his heel, and abruptly left. I quickly scanned the papers looking for what we were being sued for and the amount: negligent hiring, and the amount was for $6,000,000. That got my attention. We won the case, but the experience has stayed with me, reminding me of the importance of exercising due diligence when hiring.[2]

Negligent hiring is a tort in which an employer, a school district for example, hires an employee who then injures a third party. If the employer failed to use due diligence in the hiring process, a suit for negligent hiring may be successfully brought against the school district. "Such negligence usually consists of hiring or retaining the employee with knowledge of his unfitness, or failing to use reasonable care to discover it before hiring or retaining him."[3] This action is distinct from employment discrimination. Employment discrimination basically asserts that the reason that you did not hire me was that you discriminated against me. Negligent hiring asserts that the employer negligently hired the wrong person and that negligence resulted in an injury to me.

Beck writes that in order to establish a prima facie claim for negligent hiring the following elements must be met:

1. the defendant had a *duty* to exercise care in hiring;
2. the defendant *breached* that duty by hiring an employee who was
   a. *incompetent*, where
   b. the defendant had *notice* of the employee's incompetence; and
3. the defendant's hiring of the employee was a *proximate cause* of the plaintiff's injury.[4]

The prima facie case for negligent hiring follows the elements of the negligence torts discussed earlier.

For example, a school district hires a bus driver and does not check with the last employer as a reference. The bus driver after several uneventful months hits a student who has thrown an object on the bus and acted disrespectfully toward the bus driver. The parents sue the school district for negligent hiring, among other causes of action. The parents allege that the school district either knew or should have known that the bus driver had been suspended twice for hitting students and had suspected child abuse charges filed in response to his actions. In this case, the issue is whether the school district acted reasonably in hiring the bus driver. Would the reasonable educator have checked with the previous employer regarding the bus driver's employment history? Would due diligence in the hiring process revealed a propensity to violent responses?

Negligent hiring lawsuits "have increased significantly over the last few years."[5] While principals typically do not possess the final hiring authority, they are often involved in hiring decisions. It is best to develop an understanding of negligent hiring as a hedge against lawsuits naming the principal as one of the defendants. In some states and school districts principals have expanded authority to hire employees. This increased authority has corresponding responsibility attached to it.

Negligent hiring applies to *all* employees who are hired, not just teachers. Due diligence must be exercised when hiring the lunch duty supervisor, the substitute teacher, or a substitute custodian, as well as the bus driver, school secretary, and classroom teacher.

Employers, such as school districts, are faced with a dilemma: "They are forbidden by law from asking a prospective employee certain questions, yet they can be sued for negligent hiring or retention of a dangerous employee."[6] For example, California Labor Code Section 432.7 prohibits an employer from asking an applicant for any information regarding an arrest that did not result in a conviction. In spite of the hurdles, there are steps that a school district and a principal can take to reduce the likelihood of a negligent hiring action being successful. "The key element is whether the hiring process was diligent enough to reveal any reasonably foreseeable risk of harm that a prospective . . . employee may present to students or other third parties."[7]

A prudent principal should review the employment application sections, the interview process, and the preemployment investigation. Some suggestions are offered below.[8]

Sample Employment Application Sections

- My signature below authorizes the school district to conduct a background investigation and authorizes release of information in connection with my application for employment.
- Have you ever been refused tenure or a continuing contract?
- Have you been discharged, suspended, or requested to resign from a position?
- Have you ever had a certificate or license revoked or suspended?
- Are any criminal charges or proceedings pending against you?[9]
- Has any court ever received a plea of guilty or a plea of nolo contendere from you for any offense involving moral turpitude (defined as an act of baseness, vileness, or depravity in the private and social duties that a person owes another member of society in general and that is contrary to the accepted rule of right and duty between persons), deferred further proceedings without entering a finding of guilty, or placed you on probation?[10]
- I certify that I have made true, correct, and complete answers and statements on this application in the knowledge that they may be relied upon in considering my application, and I understand that any material omission or falsely answered question made by me on this application or any supplement to it will be sufficient grounds for failure to employ me or for my discharge should I become employed with the school district.

Interview[11]

- It is best to use an interviewing team so as to provide a variety of perspectives on the applicant's skills, knowledge, and demeanor.
- The interview team must be fully knowledgeable about the requirements for the position.
- Only those applicants that meet *all* of the requirements for the position should be invited to an interview.

Sample Preemployment Investigation for a Teacher

- Before a contract is offered, an administrator, or principal if applicable, from the personnel department must call the previous employer/principal or, if the candidate is a new teacher, the master teacher or university supervisor to do a reference check.
- A written record of who conducted the preemployment investigation, who the investigator spoke to, and the date and time of the contact should be kept. The record can be kept in the personnel file if hired and confidentiality can be maintained since it is a preemployment inquiry.
- Unless some specific questions arise during the interview, the investigator could ask the following questions from a prepared form and record the responses:

  What is your name and position?
  How long have you been acquainted with the applicant?
  In what capacity did you know the applicant?
  Did you directly supervise or observe the applicant performing his/her duties?
  What are the strengths of the applicant?
  How would you characterize the applicant's relationship with his/her students?
  If we hire this applicant, in what area would you suggest that we provide additional inservicing or training?
  Have there been any investigations concerning unprofessional conduct, incompetence, insubordination, or immorality concerning this applicant?
  Would you rehire this individual if given the chance?

- Conduct any fingerprint and/or criminal background investigations that are available in your state.

- If any questions arise from the investigation, check further before offering a contract.

There are no magic formulas that can be written or incantations that can be invoked that will guarantee immunity from lawsuits. The decision to hire a specific teacher or employee may well be one of the most important decisions made by principals and other administrators. The people in our schools make the school what it is and what it can become. Time, commitment, and knowledge must be invested in this crucial decision, not just to avoid liability but to secure the professional services of the best teachers available. Our students deserve no less effort on our part.

NOTES

1. "A necessary element of a cause of action for negligent hiring is that the employer knew or should have known of an employee's propensity for the conduct that caused the injury" (C.M. v. City of New York, 800 N.Y.S.2d 898, 901 (Sup. 2005)).

2. We were sued because a high school teacher that we hired two years prior had been arrested for the sexual abuse of one of our students. We acted prudently by checking with the teacher's previous school district about his qualifications. The school district had not revealed that the teacher had been investigated several times for alleged unprofessional conduct with students. That school district settled with the parents, who brought suit against us for an undisclosed amount.

3. 53 Am. Jur. 2d Master and Servant, Sec. 422 (1970).

4. Jeremy Beck, "Entity Liability for Teacher-on-Student Sexual Harassment: Could State Law Offer Greater Protection Than Federal Statutes?" 35 *Journal of Law & Education* 141 (2006) (emphasis in original).

5. Daniel Feldman, "Employment Law Update," May 23, 2002. Site accessed 8/25/05, www.imakenews.com/employmentlaw/e article000072814.cfm.

6. VeriRes: A Nationwide Employment Screening Service, "A Look at Negligent Hiring Law Suits." Site visited 8/25/05, www.verires.com/nhiring.htm.

7. Todd A. DeMitchell, "School District Liability for Negligent Hiring," *International Journal of Educational Reform*, 1993 at 183.

8. These suggestions are adapted from Todd A. DeMitchell, "School District Liability for Negligent Hiring," *supra*.

9. American Association of School Personnel Administrators, *Model Application Project* (1989).

10. J. L. Horton and V. Corcoran, *Preemployment Inquiries: Avoiding Pitfalls in the Hiring Process* (1985).

11. Some questions should not be asked in an interview because they are discriminatory or not job related. For example, these types of questions cannot be asked:

- You have a distinctive accent. Are you Asian?
- Day care is difficult to find in our area. How will you provide for the care of your children?
- Could we help you get in touch with a rabbi to help you make contact with our Jewish community?
- Will your physical disability allow you to do this job?
- Are you planning on starting a family soon?

8

Educational Malpractice

Terri A. DeMitchell, J.D., M.A., M.Ed.

One of the easiest questions to answer while working as a school law attorney representing California school districts was: "A parent has threatened to file a lawsuit alleging that we did not properly educate her child. Are we in trouble?" The answer was a simple no. Lawsuits for educational malpractice have not prevailed. While professionals, such as physicians and attorneys,[1] are held individually accountable through malpractice suits when their professional actions fail to conform to accepted practices and an injury results, to date, malpractice in education has failed as a theory of recovery.[2] Currently, educators are not required, as other professionals are required, to perform their duties in accordance with the standard of care observed by their profession.[3] Administrative action can be taken resulting in an educator being disciplined, even dismissed, for incompetence. But a student who is injured due to an inadequate education[4] has no legal recourse in a suit for damages. In fact, in most jurisdictions, a suit for educational malpractice is against public policy.

Even though the question about educational malpractice is easy to answer now, educational leaders should understand the concept because malpractice may become a viable tort in the future. This possibility increases as accountability tightens its hold on education, teaching becomes more scripted, and legislation such as No Child Left Behind defines an adequate education and mandate that only "highly qualified teachers" may teach in our public school classrooms.

A debate that is reshaping the landscape of public education is how best to reform education. The emergence of reform strategies is in response to the public's desire to hold the public schools accountable for the education of society's youth. "The formulation of standards and the measurement of performance [are] intended to tidy up a messy system and to make teachers and school administrators truly accountable."[5] Nearly all states have instituted some form of an accountability mechanism.

Currently, high stakes testing of students is the dominant form of accountability. But failure of such tests can have different consequences. According to one type of accountability policy, if a student fails the exit examination the student cannot graduate even if he or she has passed every class, including the in-class tests.[6] Therefore, the student suffers the direct consequences for failing the high-stakes test and is held personally accountable—no graduation, no social promotion. Another accountability policy involves holding the school accountable for the failure of students to reach the prescribed competence level. No Child Left Behind is one such accountability policy.[7] If a school is considered failing, allow students to escape to another school, fire the principal, or reconstitute the school.

The student is held responsible under one accountability policy. The school is held accountable under the second. Can a policy directed at holding the teacher accountable be far behind? In an era of educational accountability, is it time to revisit the viability of the accountability system of professional malpractice?

MALPRACTICE IN THE PROFESSIONS

> If doctors, lawyers, architects, engineers, and other professionals are charged with a duty owing to the public whom they serve, it could not be said that nothing in the law precludes similar treatment of professional educators. (Donohue v. Copiague Union Free School District)[8]

Professionals who engage in alleged professional misconduct or who allegedly lack appropriate skill resulting in injury may be liable for malpractice. Malpractice is often distinguished from other wrongs committed by professionals in that it deals with the quality of the services rendered.[9] Professionals are held accountable through malpractice "for failure to perform in accordance with skills that define their jobs."[10] Professionals are expected to utilize a standard of care recognized by their profession as appropriate, based on the training received and the commonly held set of practices associated with the service rendered.[11] Failure to exercise the accepted standard of care may form the basis for malpractice if the negligent delivery of the service is the legal cause for an injury suffered due to the lack of an appropriate standard of care.

In medicine, a surgeon may operate on a patient and follow all of the commonly accepted procedures for the operation, and yet the patient may die. The death of the patient is not the measure of malpractice; the delivery of the standard of care concerning the operation is instead dispositive. In other words, a malpractice suit will not prevail if the patient dies in spite of the surgeon doing everything expected in the delivery of the professional service. In legal malpractice, lawyers may not be responsible for honest errors of judgment.[12]

MALPRACTICE IN EDUCATION

In the landmark 1976 case *Peter W. v. San Francisco Unified School District*, the issue of educational malpractice was first adjudicated.[13] This case set the stage for all subsequent educational malpractice actions by clearly denying recovery. In this case, a high school graduate brought suit against the San Francisco Unified School District, the superintendent, and governing board to recover for alleged negligence in instruction and intentional misrepresentation of the student's progress. The plaintiff claimed that these actions resulted in depriving him of basic academic skills. In other words, he asserted that he was injured because he had not been adequately educated.

The plaintiff in this action was an eighteen-year-old male who had recently graduated from the San Francisco Unified School District after having been enrolled in the school system for a period of approximately twelve years. He claimed that although he had graduated from high school he possessed only a fifth-grade reading ability.

The plaintiff alleged, in part, that the four requisite elements (duty owed, breach of duty, causation, and sufficient injury) for bringing an action in tort were present in his case. In his complaint, the plaintiff alleged that the defendant school district, which includes its agents and employees, had a duty to provide plaintiff with an adequate education and that the defendant breached that duty. In addition, the plaintiff alleged that this breach of duty was in fact the proximate cause of plaintiff's inability to read at grade level and that the plaintiff had been injured because of this inability.

At the outset, the court's opinion acknowledged that the parties to the action did not debate the adequacy of the plaintiff's claim with respect to negligent acts, proximate cause, and injury, therefore clearly recognizing most of the required elements in a tort suit. The court, however, had very serious reservations regarding the elements of standard of care, causation, and injury, which resulted in a determination that educators owed no duty of care to students despite the fact that such a duty is readily recognized in suits against other professionals.

Peter W. offered three theories to support his contention that a duty of care existed: 1) assumption of the function of instruction of students imposes the duty to exercise reasonable care in its discharge; 2) there is a special relationship between students and teachers that supports the teachers' duty to exercise reasonable care; and 3) the duty of teachers is to exercise reasonable care in instruction and supervision of students in California as set forth in judicial decisions.

The court admitted that the facts impose upon the defendant a duty of care within the common meaning of the term. However, the court dismissed each of the theories raised by the plaintiff for want of relevant authority establishing that the enrollment of the plaintiff in defendants' schools creates a legal duty, which will sustain liability for negligence of its breach. The most pertinent principle for purposes of this issue expounded by the court was that "judicial recognition of such duty in the defendant, with the consequence of his liability in negligence for its breach, is initially to be dictated or precluded by considerations of public policy."[14]

Despite the constraints placed on expanding the concept of duty, the court acknowledged that the California Supreme Court has in the past opened or sanctioned new areas of tort liability when the wrongs and the injuries involved were both comprehensible and assessable within the existing legal framework. However, the court in *Peter W.* was unwilling to extend the concept of a duty of due care to the facts presented in this case due to a belief that there is no recognizable standard of care, cause, or injury in education:

> Unlike the activity of the highway or the marketplace, classroom methodology affords no readily acceptable standards of care, or

> cause, or injury. The science of pedagogy itself is fraught with different and conflicting theories of how or what a child should be taught, and any layman might—and commonly does—have his own emphatic views on the subject. The "injury" claimed here is the plaintiff's inability to read and write. Substantial professional authority attests that the achievement of literacy in the schools, or its failure, is influenced by a host of factors which affect the pupil subjectively, from outside the formal teaching process, and beyond the control of its ministers. They may be physical, neurological, emotional, cultural, and environmental; they may be present but not perceived, recognized but not identified.[15]

Based on the above reasoning, the court found that a duty of due care should not be created because of the multiple factors involved in education and because of an assumption on the part of the court that there is no recognized methodology with regard to education. However, the court expressed other concerns that help explain its reluctance to allow a cause of action for educational malpractice that extended beyond the four elements required for a negligence case. In closing its opinion the court explained:

> To hold them to an actionable "duty of care," in the discharge of their academic functions would expose them to the tort claims—real or imagined—of disaffected students and parents in countless numbers. They are already beset by social and financial problems which have gone to major litigation, but for which no permanent solution has yet appeared. The ultimate consequences, in terms of public time and money, would burden them—and society—beyond calculation.
>
> Upon consideration of the role imposed upon the public schools by law and the limitations imposed upon them by their publicly-supported budgets and of the just-cited "consequences to the community of imposing [upon them] a duty to exercise care with resulting liability for breach" we find no such "duty" in . . . plaintiff's complaint.[16]

Thus, the plaintiff's action failed because the court refused to find that a California school district owed a duty of care while instructing students. According to California law, educators must adequately supervise students,[17] but according to *Peter W.* they do not have a duty to adequately educate them.

Three years after the case of *Peter W.* was heard in California, a high school student in New York brought a similar action. In *Donohue v. Copiague Union Free School District*,[18] the plaintiff alleged that he had attended Copiague Senior High School from 1972 to 1976, when he graduated without the rudimentary ability to read and write. The plaintiff in this case sought $5,000,000 in damages.

The plaintiff asserted two causes of action. The first was educational malpractice and the second was the negligent breach of a constitutionally imposed duty to educate under New York law.

The court rejected the second claim with very little discussion. However, the first cause of action, alleging educational malpractice, was analyzed in depth. The court found that such a cause of action was indeed plausible and stated that the "the imagination need not be overly taxed to envision allegations of a legal duty of care flowing from educators. . . ."[19]

However, after determining that a cause of action in educational malpractice was indeed possible, the court opined that such claims should not be entertained for public policy reasons. The court found that the control and management of educational affairs in the state of New York was vested in the Board of Regents and the Commissioner of Education and that the courts should not interfere with the decision making of that entity absent a gross violation of public policy. The court did not, however, elaborate on what type of violation might be considered gross, but clearly a lack of due care while instructing students was not considered a gross violation of public policy. Specifically the court held that:

> To entertain a cause of action for "educational malpractice" would require the courts not merely to make judgments as to the validity of the broad educational policies—a course we have unfalteringly eschewed in the past—but, more importantly, to sit in review of the day-to-day implementation of these policies. Recognition in the courts of this cause of action would constitute blatant interference with the responsibility for the administration of the public school system lodged by Constitution and statute in school administrative agencies.[20]

Whereas the court in *Peter W.* found that no duty of care exists in the educational setting, and therefore an action in malpractice is not possible, the *Donohue* court found that the four elements of a tort do exist in educational malpractice cases. However, the court in *Donohue* chose to insulate educators from liability as a matter of public policy by deferring to the judgment of the professionals. Interestingly, in medical and legal malpractice cases, the courts defer to the profession only to establish a standard of care, not to insulate the professionals from accountability. Thus, the courts believe that educators should not be held accountable for the services they render for both legal and policy reasons.

DEFENSES TO MALPRACTICE

If a patient has contributed to his or her injuries or has assumed some sort of risk, damages will not be awarded or will be reduced. The courts have held that the creation of a physician-patient relationship requires that the duty established be reciprocal. Thus, the patient is required to use the care a person would ordinarily use in similar circumstances and if he or she does not, then the patient cannot hold the physician liable for harm. Specifically, a patient is required to provide adequate information to the physician, follow the instructions given by the physician, and submit to the treatment the physician orders. If failure to do so enhances the injury, the patient will not be able to recover damages for his contribution to the injury.

For example, in an action against a physician for the improper diagnosis of appendicitis, the court held the plaintiff contributorily negligent for failing to disclose pertinent information to the physician and for failing to seek further medical attention when her condition worsened.[21] In another case, a patient was determined to be contributorily negligent when her physician told her to return in six months after a lump was found in her breast and she waited fifteen months, resulting in a loss of survival expectancy.[22]

Since educational malpractice is not recognized as a cause of action, the issue of defenses has not been addressed in the case law. However, discussion of factors regarding causation, such as motivation and home life discussed previously, could be raised as a defense since these are external factors beyond the control of the educator. The classic defense of contributory negligence on the part of the plaintiff would be available in an educational malpractice suit as it is in medical malpractice. It is clear that a physician would not be held liable for damages if a diabetic would not take her insulin even though it was prescribed and the ramifications for not taking the medication were discussed. This defense could be raised when the student failed to follow the instructions of the teacher, such as not turning in assignments or turning in partially completed assignments, or when a student failed to pay attention in class. Therefore, a student would arguably be required to take reasonable responsibility for his or her own learning.

Patients die and clients go to jail. The outcome of the rendering of professional services is not always positive. The courts recognize that part of being a professional includes making judgment calls that may not always guarantee a positive result. The issue, generally, is whether or not the professional rendered the expected service. Following the examples from medicine and law, the issue would not be whether the student learned but whether the educator rendered the instruction that would be expected of a professional educator.

CONCLUSION

To date, educators have not been held legally accountable for the professional services they render. The duty owed analysis in *Peter W.* concluded that as educators we do not have standards of practice that guide our teaching. However, a sea change may be occurring in which educators may be held liable for the performance of their professional activities. We have standards for students and standards for curricula. We are developing sets of standards for teaching through the National Board for Professional Teaching Standards,[23] research, and interstate compacts. Most professional associations have defined in various terms of vagueness what a teacher should do as a demonstration of best practices. David Dill writes of the time following *Peter W.* that "[o]ne distinguishing characteristic of the education reform movement of the 1980s is the assumption that a knowledge base for the teaching profession now can be defined—a knowledge base that can be used in designing future teachers education programs."[24] Books such as *Qualities of Effective Teachers*, which discusses a research-based framework for quality teaching, have become commonplace in the educational lexicon.[25] And, research on best practices in teaching is discussed in books as well as appearing in scholarly compendiums.[26]

Parker identifies another aspect of how a duty to teach is formed. He writes, "Some state legislatures have also created Professional Teaching Practices Commissions that are responsible for developing through the teaching profession, criteria of professional practice, including professional performance."[27] Arguably, there is a body of professional knowledge gained through research and collective professional wisdom that is accepted by the various professional organizations that define what instructional duty is owed to students.

Accountability measures are sweeping the nation. A cause of action for educational malpractice grounded in accountability and supported by a growing body of best practices research, which defines professional practice, may reverse the history of court aversion to the tort. Furthermore, while suits against school districts for educational malpractice have not prevailed in the courts, some suits against individuals for professional malpractice have had some limited success. These cases differ from educational malpractice in that academic/curricular decisions or instructional deficiencies are not questioned. Rather, the claim is that "specific individuals have negligently performed their professional duties."[28] Consequently, the confluence of strengthened standards and individual professional malpractice may be moving public education down the path toward educational malpractice. Should this come to pass, educators, including principals, will need to understand the ramifications of this new duty owed to students so that decisions can be made to avoid liability.

NOTES

1. *See,* Michael J. Polelle, "Who's on First, and What's a Professional," 33 *University of South Florida Law Review* 205, 206 (1999). ("Judicial intervention in the specific professions of medicine and law has largely molded the malpractice law applied to all professionals.")

2. *See,* Ross v. Creighton University, 740 F.Supp. 1319, 1327 (N.D. Ill. 1990) ("Educational malpractice is a tort theory beloved of commentators, but not of courts."); Livosi v. Hicksville Union-Free School Dist., 693 N.Y.S.2d 617, 617–618 (1999) ("As a matter of public policy, such a cause of action cannot be entertained by courts of this State."); and Brown v. Compton Unif. Sch. Dist., 80 Cal. Rptr2d 171, 172 (App. 2d Dist. 1998) ("Policy considerations preclude 'an actionable duty of care' in persons and agencies who administer the academic phases of the public educational process,") (citing Peter W. v. San Francisco Unif. Sch. Dist., 131 Cal. Rptr, 854, 861 (App. 1st Dist. 1976)).

3. For example, The Model Rules of Professional Conduct (2002 edition), paragraph 4, states in part, "in all professional functions a lawyer should be competent, prompt, and diligent." And Rule 1.1 of the same document states that competence requires a lawyer to employ and maintain "the requisite knowledge and skill." Center for Professional Responsibility, American Bar Association. Site accessed 9/28/02, www.abanet.org/cpr/mrpc.

4. Michael Smoker, *Results: The Key to Continuous School Improvement,* 8 (1996) ("A report on education and the economy indicates that educational attainment is the single most determinant of a person's success in the labor market. The 50 years it has been tracked, the payoff to schooling has never been higher.").

5. Elliot W. Eisner. "What Does It Mean to Say a School Is Doing Well?" *Phi Delta Kappan* 82: 367 (2001).

6. *See,* Rebecca R. Glasgow, "Notes and Comments:, Can Students Sue When Schools Don't Make the Grade? The Washington Assessment of Student Learning and Educational Malpractice," 76 *Washington Law Review* 893, 925 (2001). Students who fail the Washington Assessment of Student Learning test but have met all graduation requirements should be able to bring a private cause of action for educational malpractice. "The [Academic Achievement and Accountability] Statute expresses a clear school district duty to individual students while insisting on school accountability."

7. No Child Left Behind (P.L. 107-110 (H.R. 1)) lists consequences for failure to make adequate yearly progress. Site accessed 12/26/05, www.ed.gov/news/letters/020724.html.

8. 391 N.E.2d 1352, 1353 (1979).

9. Ronald E. Mallen, "Recognizing and Defending Legal Malpractice," 20 *Southern California Law Review* 203 (1979).

10. John G. Culhane, "Reinvigorating Educational Malpractice Claims: A Representational Focus," 67 *Washington Law Review* 349, 372 (1992).

11. For example, a physician owes a patient (1) the duty to possess the requisite knowledge and skill such as is possessed by the average member of the medical profession, (2) the duty to exercise ordinary and reasonable care in the application of such knowledge and skill, and (3) the duty to use best judgment in such application (61 AM. JUR. 2d Physicians and Surgeons, Etc. 311 (1981)).

12. Mark Richard Cummsford, "Resolving Fee Disputes and Legal Malpractice Claims Using ADR," 85 *Marquette Law Review* 975, 978 (2002).

13. 60 Cal.App. 3rd 814 (Ct.App. 1976).

14. *Id.* at 822.

15. *Id.* at 824.

16. *Id.* at 825.

17. CA. Educ. Code §44807.

18. 391 N.E.2d 1352 (1979).

19. *Id.* at 1353.

20. *Id.* at 1354 (citations omitted).

21. Carreker v. Harper, 396 S.E.2d 587 (1990).

22. Roers v. Engebretson, 479 N.W.2d 422 (Minn.1992).

23. For information on the National Board for Professional Teaching Standards visit www.nbpts.org.

24. David D. Dill and Associates, *What Teachers Need to Know: The Knowledge, Skills, and Values Essential to Good Teaching*, xiii (1990).

25. James H. Stronge, *Qualities of Effective Teachers*, (2002).

26. *See*, M. L. Wittrock (Ed.), *Handbook of Research on Teaching* (3rd ed. 1986).

27. Johnny C. Parker, "Educational Malpractice: A Tort Is Born," 39 *Cleveland State Law Review* 301, 318 (1991).

28. Julie Underwood and L. Dean Webb, *School Law for Teachers: Concepts and Applications*, 108 (2006). *See*, Sain v. Cedar Rapids Community School District, 626 N.W.2d 115 (Iowa 2001), in which a school counselor gave wrong information regarding an English core course needed for Division I NCAA basketball eligibility. The student, as a result of the information provided by the counselor, lost his college scholarship. The student sued and won on the basis of negligent misrepresentation. The student relied on the advice when the counselor knew or should have known that it was wrong. However, not all similar misadvising cases resulted in a win for the defendant (Scott v. Savers Property and Casualty Insurance Co, 663 N.W.2d 715 (Wis. 2003)); Brown v. Compton Unified School District, 80 Cal. Rptr. 2d 171 (1998)).

9

Sexual Abuse of Students: Case Studies on Liability

It seems axiomatic that students should be able to attend school and not have to run a gauntlet of abuse. Unfortunately, the school as a safe harbor is not always safe for students. All too often students suffer harassment, abuse, and sexual assault while at school or while participating in school-related activities. While there are protections for students codified in various federal statutes (for example, Title IX[1] and Section 1983[2]), this discussion is limited to those instances when the school, through its employees, negligently supervises either teachers or students and a student is harmed. A discussion of the protections afforded to students under the federal statutes is important for a school leader to know, but they must be left for another day and another book.

OFF SCHOOL GROUNDS

K.C. was a female twelve-year-old junior high school student in Opelousas, Louisiana. It was K.C's. first year at the school, and the school year had just begun when the vice principal, Mr. Hooks, informed her that her skirt was too short and violated the school dress code. She was sent to the office to call someone to bring her some acceptable clothes. Ms. Guilbeau, the school secretary, allowed K.C. to use the phone to call home.

K.C. called home and spoke to her eighteen-year-old brother. Her brother told her that he did not have any transportation and, therefore, could not bring her any clothing. K.C. told Ms. Guilbeau that to obtain appropriate clothing she would have to go home and change. According to K.C., Ms. Guilbeau pushed the checkout sheet toward her and told her to check out. The checkout sheet showed that K.C. left the school at 7:59 a.m. K.C. walked home alone through an area called "the Hill" and known for illicit drug and other activities. Eight blocks from the school K.C. encountered Neil Mark Lewis, who sexually molested her.

K.C. brought suit against the school district and won. The trial court found that the defendant owed a duty of reasonable supervision, which extended to an indecent act that occurred approximately eight blocks from the school. The court held that the school breached its duty of reasonable supervision. K.C. was awarded $405 in medical expenses and $20,000 in general damages. The school district appealed the decision of the trial court.[3]

The court of appeals noted that allowing K.C. to check herself out violated school policy. School policy required that school personnel make some contact with a child's parent before the child could leave campus. In the event that a parent could not be contacted, the "proper thing to do would be to have the child remain in the office or return to class until such contact could be made."[4] In the alternative, a student could be checked out of school with parental approval confirmed by direct contact by the principal or vice principal with the parent giving permission. Adding to the finding of negligence, the vice principal did not inquire as to what happened to K.C. once he returned to the office.

Ms. Guilbeau, the school secretary, acknowledged that K.C.'s phone call to her brother did not rise to the level justifying her departure. Because Ms. Guilbeau did not involve herself in school disciplinary problems, "Ms. Guilbeau simply did not consider K.C. to be her responsibility under these circumstances." One school employee did not consider it her responsibility to implement the school policy, and the other school employee did not check on the student he had sent to the office. But both employees stated that they would not want their daughter walking alone on the streets of "the Hill."

Duty Owed

The court of appeals held that the school owed a duty of reasonable supervision while a student is on campus during regular school hours.

"Certainly, included within that duty of reasonable supervision includes the duty to make the appropriate supervisory decisions concerning a student's departure from campus during regular school hours."[5]

Breach of Duty

The defendants "breached their duty to K.C. by violating their own policy."[6] A reasonable educator/employee would not have violated the stated policy on sending students home alone.

Causation

"Clearly, K.C. would not have been sexually molested had she not been allowed to leave the junior high school campus."[7] Continuing the causation analysis, "[w]e find that a causal connection exists between her lack of supervision and the incident giving rise to her injury. We further find that the incident would not have occurred but for the absence of the appropriate degree of care and supervision required under the facts of the case at bar."[8]

Sufficient Injury

Dr. Pryer, a clinical psychologist who treated K.C., testified that K.C. had nightmares, that her classmates "teased her unmercifully" after learning of the incident, wished that she were dead so that she could escape the teasing, was mildly depressed and anxious, and was very angry. K.C. was injured.

As seen in this case, just having a policy is not enough—it must also be followed. The school employees stated that they would not have allowed their daughters to walk alone in the neighborhood where K.C. walked home alone and was molested. The crush of the daily work and the statement that it was "not my responsibility" ring hollow in light of the sexual assault of a student, which could have been avoided.

ON THE SCHOOL BUS

Jane Doe and Mary Doe, twin sixteen-year-old students, were passengers on a school bus that took them to a high school basketball game in Springhill, Louisiana. In addition to Jane and Mary, the bus carried the male and female basketball teams and their two coaches. On the trip to the game one coach (Hall) sat in the front of the bus and the other (Locke) sat between the boys and the girls. Coach Locke soon shifted seats to the front of the bus and asked Jane Doe to switch seats so that the student who was originally sitting with her could sit with her once again. Jane Doe took the coach's seat, which was located right before the section occupied by the boys.

For the return trip Jane sat in the same seat near the boys and the two coaches sat up front. This was in violation of a strict school policy that required that the boys' team be physically separated from the girls' team and that the coaches be positioned between the girls' and boys' teams while the bus was in transit. The policy was originally enacted because of prior sexual misconduct on school buses.

At some point Coach Hall apparently fell asleep. During the return trip, some unspecified sexual contact took place between Jane Doe and five male basketball players.[9] Although a number of students on the bus were aware of the sexual assault as it was occurring, the coaches were not made aware of it until the following Monday when some of the female players informed their coach. A full investigation was initiated right away. The five male students were expelled from school. Approximately six months later suit was brought for negligent supervision.

The school board was found liable for the sexual battery of Jane Doe. Jane Doe was awarded $50,000 in damages for past and future physical pain and suffering, $150,000 for past and future mental anguish, and $50,000 for past and future loss of enjoyment of life. In addition, Mary Doe and the twins' father, John Doe, were each awarded $10,000 in damages for loss of consortium. The school district appealed the verdict.[10] The plaintiffs won on appeal.

Duty Owed

"Acting *in loco parentis,* the coaches, as empowered representatives of the high school and School Board staff, had a duty to monitor the students under their supervision with reasonable care."[11] The duty owed to Jane Doe specifically entailed a separation on the school bus between the boys and the girls with the placement of adult coaches between the two groups.

Breach of Duty

The coaches failed to follow the policy of separation. "Although the coaches testified that they were unaware of this policy, apparently the jury found their testimony lacking in credibility."[12] The coaches began the trip with separation between the girls and the boys because Coach Locke was seated between them but later moved to the front of the bus. A reasonable coach would have followed the policy separation. The coaches acted unreasonably by not following the policy, thus their duty to Jane Doe was breached. The sexual activity was not "a spontaneous act" that could not have been prevented. The court held that "this sexual incident could have been easily avoided."[13]

Causation

It was foreseeable that this type of injury could occur on a school bus because the policy acknowledged the likelihood of such acts and took reasonable steps to reduce the instance of injury. "There is no question that 'but for' placing an emotionally immature minor in a position of close proximity to the boys and failing to properly supervise the students in their charge by either not paying close attention or even staying awake while on duty, the injuries sustained by Jane Doe would not have occurred."[14]

Sufficient Injury

The court found that Jane Doe suffered a sufficient injury to warrant an award of damages.

The court of appeals did not mince words about the actions of the coaches. It stated, "We find that the lack of supervision in this case was reprehensible."[15] It is clear that the coaches breached their duty to Jane Doe. We are left with the question of how appropriately the principal discharged the duty he or she owed to Jane. Did the principal review the policy with the coaches on a regular basis? How often was the policy discussed with the individuals assigned to its implementation? Was the policy in writing and accessible to the coaches who would travel with their teams?

EDUCATORS

The taboos regarding the sexual abuse of children who are subject to the control of a parent are similar to the taboo of the sexual abuse of a student by an educator who stands in the place of the parent. Richard Riley, the former U.S. secretary of education, summed it up nicely when he stated, "Any sexual harassment of a student —particularly sexual abuse by a teacher—is a basic breach of trust between the school and the student and family."[16] However, the degree of legal protection offered to students who are sexually abused by their teachers or administrators may not be up to the challenge of protecting students from abusive employees.[17]

Most sexual abuse of students perpetrated by school employees occurs in closed classrooms and away from school. Consequently, the signs, which would give rise to foreseeability of abuse, are often not visible. For example, a high school social studies teacher initiated a sexual relationship, including intercourse, with a fifteen-year-old student during the summer break.[18] While the student consented to the sex, it was statutory rape.

The teacher, Joel Barsky, had a valid teaching credential, he had no criminal record for sexual misconduct, he received satisfactory evaluations, and the principal never observed Barsky involved in inappropriate behavior with students nor did the principal receive any complaints about Barsky. The court held that the school had not received any notice of Barsky engaging in any misconduct. In other words, the school had no foreseeability that Barsky posed a sexual risk to the plaintiff student. If there was no foreseeability of harm, the school had no heightened duty of supervision. The court asserted the following:

> Students frequently spend more waking hours with their teachers than their parents. Close bonds sometimes develop, and a caring teacher can play an important role in helping a child. That a teacher may spend a considerable amount of time with a student does not prove that the teacher is engaging in misconduct. If a principal were to stop all after-class contact between teachers and students, that would interfere with the teacher-student rapport that is critical to the educational process.[19]

This case demonstrates the challenge of balancing the need for supervision of teachers to protect students from potential sexual harm with the need to allow teachers flexibility and support to develop meaningful, professional relationships with students. For many students, their teacher may be the only stable relationship in their young lives.

Professional teachers use their power to assist students. Predatory teachers abuse their power to further their own ends. Professional teachers recognize the inherent boundary limits of their relationship with students. Predatory teachers know no boundaries. The challenge for principals is to communicate the boundaries in a consistent, clear manner and then pursue any potential transgressions with interviews and observations.

Mary Jo McGrath, a national expert on teacher conduct, offers several important considerations for principals supervising employees. She writes the following:

> State courts often award money damages in cases involving various administrators' duties, such as:
>
> - Failure to supervise. An administrator owes a legal duty to the students to provide adequate supervision of school employees. This includes appropriate observation, investigation, correction of improper conduct, adequate documentation, and discipline.
> - Failure to investigate. Failure to investigate or a perfunctory or inadequate investigation of rumors, reports, or complaints of sexual misconduct or of suspicious conduct by a school employee may constitute negligence by an administrator.
> - Failure to train. Supervisors have a duty to adopt and enforce appropriate policies and to train teachers, guidance counselors, school nurses, and administrators to respond adequately to signs, reports, and complaints of sexual misconduct to protect students.
> - Failure to hire carefully.[20]

A QUESTIONABLE DEFENSE

Earlier we discussed the defenses to a tort. Once the plaintiff has established the prima facie case (duty owed, breach, causation, and injury) the defendant has the opportunity to respond to the allegations. However, a defendant may in a responsive pleading assert an affirmative defense. Several defenses are available to a defendant: accidents/acts of God, immunity, assumption of the risk, contributory negligence, and comparative negligence. An affirmative defense includes assumption of risk and contributory negligence in addition to other defenses. This section explores the use of the defense of contributory negligence asserted by a school district when one of its teachers sexually abused a child.

Leslie was a thirteen-year-old student and Steven Diaz was a teacher at her middle school. In 2001, they engaged in sexual activity in Diaz's classroom on four different occasions. Leslie and her parents later brought suit against Diaz, the principal, and the school district.[21] They alleged that Diaz sexually abused Leslie and the school district and its principal were negligent in hiring and supervising Diaz.

The school district asserted an affirmative defense stating that Leslie had voluntarily participated in the "sexual relationship," which constituted contributory negligence. Leslie and her parents moved for partial summary judgment seeking to strike the affirmative defense. The Supreme Court of Washington meeting en banc addressed the following certified question from the U.S. District Court of Washington:

> Many a 13 year old victim of sexual abuse by her teacher on school premises, who brings a negligence action against the school district and her principal for failure to supervise or for the negligent hiring of the teacher, have contributory [negligence] assessed against her under Washington Tort Reform Act for her participation in the relationship.[22]

The defendant school district and principal asserted that Washington had a long history of holding children responsible for contributory negligence and that "Leslie had a duty to protect herself against sexual abuse but failed to do so."[23] According to the defendant's argument Leslie should have stopped the sexual abuse. In other words, the thirteen-year-old student, who was not old enough to give legal consent for sexual activity and was in a subservient role to her teacher, had a duty to stop the sexual abuse. The affirmative defense of contributory negligence argues that Leslie failed to "exercise reasonable care or otherwise avoid the injury."[24]

The Washington court held that "a defense of contributory negligence should not be available to the perpetrator[25] of sexual abuse or to a third party that is in a position to control the perpetrator." The court recognized the vulnerability of children in a school setting and that as a matter of public policy children do not have a duty to protect themselves from sexual abuse by their teachers. It is the educators who have the duty to protect students.[26]

The following chapter will continue the discussion of the legal protections afforded, or more precisely, not afforded to students placed in our care. It will cover such topics as the "turkey trot" and school district vicarious liability for the sexual abuse of students perpetrated by its employees.

NOTES

1. *See*, "Sexual Harassment Guidance: Harassment of Students by School Employees, Other Students or Third Parties" www.ed.gov/legislation/FedRegister/other/2000-4/110200b.html.

2. *See*, Craig v. Lima City Schools Board of Education, 384 F.Supp.2d 1136 (N.D.Ohio 2005), in which a high school teacher and coach had sexual intercourse with one of his students starting in her freshman year continuing to her junior year, resulting in her pregnancy. The student traveled with the teacher when he coached the girl's basketball team, acting as the team's statistician. The student alleged that they would sit together on the bus covered by a blanket in plain sight of everyone on the bus. "Inappropriate touching allegedly occurred during those trips and they often fell asleep leaning against each other. However, no one ever reported the behavior or took any steps to stop it," at 1141–1142.

3. D.C. v. St. Landry Parish School Board, 802 So.2d 19 (La.App. 3 Cir. 2001).

4. *Id.* at 22.

5. *Id.* at 23.

6. *Id.*

7. *Id.* at 22.

8. *Id.* at 23.

9. There was some testimony that Jane Doe willingly participated in the activity. However, the court focused on the fact that Jane Doe had an emotional make-up of a ten- to eleven-year-old child. The record also established that

she had a full-scale I.Q. of 70 to 79. The court further found that Jane Doe's maturity level and low I.Q. rendered her "easily coerced and/or intimidated." Doe, infra, note 10 at 282. Consequently, the court did not accept the argument by the school district that a sexual battery never occurred because Jane voluntarily participated in the sexual activities.

10. Doe ex rel Doe v. DeSoto Parish School Board, 907 So.2d 275 (La.App. 2 Cir. 2005).

11. *Id.* at 283.

12. *Id.* at 282.

13. *Id.*

14. *Id.* at 283.

15. *Id.*

16. Mark Walsh (1998), "Riley Restates Rules Against Harassment," *Education Week* (July 8) 1, 30 at 30.

17. *See,* Richard Fossey and Todd A. DeMitchell, "'Let the Master Answer': Holding Schools Vicariously Liable When Employees Sexually Abuse Children," 25 *Journal of Law & Education* 575 (1996), and Todd A. DeMitchell, "The Duty to Protect: Blackstone's Doctrine of In Loco Parentis. A Lens for Viewing the Sexual Abuse of Students." *Brigham Young University Education and Law Journal* 17 (2002).

18. C.M. v. City of New York, 800 N.Y.S.2d 898 (Sup. 2005).

19. *Id.* at 901.

20. Mary Jo McGrath, "The Psychodynamics of School Sexual Abuse Investigations." Site visited 12/26/05, http://mcgrathinc.com/articles-009.html.

21. Christensen v. Royal School Dist. No. 160, 124 P.3d 283 (Wash. 2005).

22. *Id.* at 284.

23. *Id.* at 286. The following cases were cited (*see,* f.n. 1 at 286): Berry v. Howe, 39 Wash.2d 235, 238 (1951) (affirming the trial court's finding that an eleven-year-old caddy was guilty of contributory negligence for failing to protect himself from being hit in the eye by a golf ball); Brown v. Derry, 10 Wash.App. 459, 464 (1974) (affirming the trial court's holding that a sixteen-year-old was guilty of contributory negligence for injuries he sustained from riding on the trunk of a moving car while wearing a wetsuit).

24. *Id.* at 288, f.n. 2.

25. *Id.* at 287.

26. "Furthermore, we have not said in this opinion that the school district should not be precluded from defending on the basis that it was not negligent. The fact that it may not, under Washington law, assert that the 13-year-old was contributorily negligent should not bar it from claiming at trial that it was careful in the hiring and the supervising of the child's teacher and, thus, was not negligent" (Id. at 288).

10

Vicarious Liability for Harm Caused by School Employees

In chapter 7 we explored the tort of negligent hiring—the hiring of an employee who poses a foreseeable risk to third parties, including students. In chapter 9 we discussed the sexual abuse of students and concluded the discussion with the need to adequately supervise our employees.[1] This chapter will continue the discussion started at the end of the last chapter on the legal limitations faced by students seeking relief from the courts for the sexual abuse caused by school employees.[2]

THE MATH TEACHER AND THE STUDENT

John R. was a ninth grade student attending a junior high school in Oakland, California. He was not a particularly strong student. In fact, his math grades were consistently low. The school had a work-experience program in which students received both school credit and monetary payments for performing such activities as grading papers. The school district allowed the work to be conducted at the teacher's home without requiring written permission from the child's parents. The program was aimed primarily at high-performing students. However, John's grades in math were not good until he took math from the same teacher that he had in the seventh grade. This male teacher asked John to participate in the work-experience program. The abrupt change in the direction of

John's grades moved one attorney to ironically call this change a "remarkable increase" in John's ability to do math.

The math teacher either encouraged or required John to come to his apartment to perform the work. After several sessions at his house the teacher sought to develop a close relationship, ultimately endeavoring to seduce John. The teacher attempted to convince John that engaging in sex acts with him would strengthen their relationship. At other times, the teacher threatened John with failing grades or that he would report that John had solicited sex from him. Eventually, John was pressured into participating in sexual acts on one occasion.

Afterwards, when John protested and told the teacher that he would report the incidents to his parents, the teacher threatened to retaliate. John was silenced by these threats and by his shame and embarrassment. Ten months later John told his father about the molestation. The sexual abuse was promptly reported to school authorities. The teacher was soon arrested.

John brought a suit against the teacher and the school district alleging that the school district was vicariously liable for the teacher's sexual abuse. We will return to John's case after we have laid a foundation for understanding how the California Supreme Court arrived at its ruling.[3]

PASSING THE TRASH AND THE TURKEY TROT

As educators we owe not only a legal duty to our students but also a professional and ethical duty as well. Unfortunately, sometimes when allegations of sexual misconduct perpetrated by school personnel are made public the immediate protection is extended to the school's reputation and its adults but not to its children.

An example of this practice may be found in Worcester, Massachusetts. A fifteen-year-old student accused her music teacher at a private school of raping her. Many in the school community did not believe the accusation. Faculty members who supported the teacher "began wearing white ribbons and a G-clef pin in a show of support for [the music teacher]" [4] Wearing the pins, in my estimation, gave tacit if not explicit official support for the teacher before the investigation had been completed. It is reasonable to imagine that it would be difficult for other students to bring complaints forward in an atmosphere where the staff openly takes sides before the facts are in. One month after the teachers began wearing pins in support of the accused music teacher, the Department of Social Services found reasonable cause that the school had "abused and neglected the [complaining] student by allowing such a hostile environment to exist".[5]

Second, even if a child or a parent reports a sexually abusive teacher, some districts try to sweep the allegation "under the rug," without notifying teacher-licensing authorities or the police. In order to save the expense of dismissal proceedings, districts often induce an accused teacher to resign by offering him a reference letter in return for waiving the right to a dismissal hearing.[6] Typically, the teacher finds a job in another district, and the truth or falsity of the allegations against him or her are never determined. An example of the "blind eye" approach to sexual abuse perpetrated by educators is found in *Gonzalez v. Yselta Independent School District*,[7] where school officials failed to report a teacher's suspected child abuse to the state Department of Human Resources as required by law. Instead, after receiving a complaint about the teacher, the school district merely moved the teacher to another school.

This practice of disposing of problem teachers, sometimes referred to as "passing the trash," is another factor that makes it difficult to assess the amount of child abuse in the schools. As Nan Stein has pointed out, the practice can lead to the creation of "mobile molesters," renegade teachers who move from district to district abusing children.[8] Others have called this practice the "dance of the lemons" and the "turkey trot."

For example, a conspiracy of silence among the teachers of a school, the abusing teacher, and the three abused students surfaced in a 1991 California case (*Daly v. Derrick*).[9] In this case a teacher at a public alternative high school sexually molested three female students from spring 1977 to spring 1978. One year after the molestations stopped, the teachers of the alternative high school and the molesting teacher met with the three abused students and reached an agreement in which the abusive teacher would transfer to another school and the students would not reveal the abuse to the school administration. The teachers were concerned that if the abuse became public knowledge the alternative high school would be closed down. In other words, the teachers considered the school more important than the students it was designed to educate and help. Can principals and other educators afford to lose sight of to whom we owe a duty of care?

Third, while legal recourse against the abuser is available to a student victim through civil and criminal actions, legal actions against the school district and its officials are much more difficult to sustain. "Although courts have been supportive of efforts by school districts to dismiss sexually abusive employees, they have not been as receptive to complaints that the abused students should be compensated."[10]

RESPONDEAT SUPERIOR: VICARIOUS LIABILITY FOR THE SERVANT'S ACTIONS

Vicarious liability of an employer for an employee's act has a long history in English law in which the master was responsible for the acts of his servants. The Latin term is *respondeat superior,* or "let the master answer." The modern justification for vicarious liability is a policy of allocation of risk. Vicarious liability is placed on the employer because, having obtained the benefits of the employee's services, the employer should bear the cost when an employee injures a third party. It is the cost of doing business because the employer is better able to absorb the costs and to distribute it through increased prices to the community at large. Employer liability extends to those acts committed within the scope of employment. As we saw earlier, school boards hold employees harmless when they are performing the work for which they were employed, even if the employee performed the work in a negligent manner.

In general, an employer will be liable for the tortuous (harmful) conduct of an employee when the employer has actual or constructive knowledge of the acts. Actual knowledge occurs when a supervisory employee has witnessed the tortuous act or actually engages in the act. An employer is also deemed to have actual knowledge if a complaint about the employee's conduct is delivered to a supervisor, especially when the employer fails to take action on the complaint. An employer is considered to have constructive knowledge of an employee's wrongful conduct if the employer could have learned about the conduct through reasonable supervision. The pervasiveness of the act may also provide the basis for an employer's constructive knowledge. For example, in *Simms v. Montgomery County Commission*, sexual harassment in the workplace was "so open and pervasive that all those in supervisory authority should have known about it."[11] Thus, the employer was held liable.

The threshold question to be asked under the doctrine of vicarious liability is whether the employee is acting within the scope of his or her employment. In other words, is the employee performing the work for which he or she was hired? Herein is the rub: teachers and other school employees are not hired to molest students. Therefore, it would appear that a school district would not be vicariously liable for the sexual assault of a student committed by one of its employees. For example, a school district was not held to be vicariously liable for a school custodian's rape of a student. The court held that there was "no work-related basis for the janitor's assault."[12]

RETURN TO *JOHN R.*

The California Supreme Court in *John R.* found three possible reasons for holding school districts liable for the sexual assault of a student by an employee and rejected all three. First, the supreme court stated that vicarious liability would likely deter school districts from authorizing or encouraging "extracurricular and/or one-on-one contacts between teachers and students or to induce districts to impose such rigorous controls on activities of this nature that the educational enterprise would be negatively affected."[13]

Second, the California high court argued that the imposition of vicarious liability on school districts for sexual abuse "would tend to make insurance, already a scarce resource, even harder to obtain, and could lead to the diversion of needed funds from the classroom to cover claims."[14] Both of these arguments are policy arguments against extending protection to students entrusted to the care of educators.

The last argument for vicarious liability is the spread of risk of loss. However, the court rejected this argument, writing:

> But the connection the authority conferred on teachers to carry out their instructional duties and the abuse of that authority to indulge in personal, sexual misconduct is simply too attenuated to deem a sexual assault as falling within the range of risks allocable to a teacher's employer. It is not a cost this particular enterprise should bear, and the consequences of imposing liability are unacceptable.[15]

Thus, the California Supreme Court declined to find a school district vicariously liable for the sexual assault of a student even though the sexual assault was facilitated by the teacher's employment, access to the student through that employment, and power over that student due to the power conferred on the teacher due to his employment as a teacher. "We think the teacher's acts here can only be characterized as 'so unusual or startling' that vicarious liability cannot fairly be imposed on the district."[16] Furthermore, on a policy basis, the court held vicarious liability would result in a "significant and unacceptable risk that school districts would be dissuaded from permitting teachers to interact with their students on any but the most formal and supervised basis."[17] Although the California Supreme Court was not willing to extend vicarious liability to school districts for basically policy reasons, the court unequivocally stated that the school district could be held liable for its own negligence. Abused students, the court opined, could pursue direct liability for negligent hiring and negligent supervision. Consequently, a finding of not holding school districts vicariously liable for the sexual assaults perpetrated by school employees did not create a safe harbor for school districts.

For example, four years after the *John R.* case, a California Court of Appeals followed the lead of its supreme court and held that a female student who was sexually molested by her teacher could not recover under vicarious liability. However, the court asserted that if the school district employees responsible for hiring and supervising the teacher knew or should have known of the teacher's prior sexual misconduct toward students, the teacher would have posed a reasonably foreseeable risk of harm, creating a duty to protect the students from such harm.[18] Schools may not be held vicariously liable for the intentional harm to students created by their employees. They may, however, be liable for their negligence in hiring and supervising the employees.

NOTES

1. "Sexual abuse of students is the No. 1 reason public school teachers have lost their licenses in West Virginia during the last five years, amounting to about 35 percent of all teaching certificates being pulled." (Associated Press, October 17, 2005, "Schools' dirty little secret," *The Charleston Gazette*. Site visited 10/17/05, http://wvgazette.com/webtools/print/news/2005101616. However, it must be noted that while this number seems high, the number of teaching credentials revoked is a relatively small percentage of the number of teaching certificates in a given state.

2. For example, in Doe v. Hillsboro Independent School District, 81 F.3d 1395 (5th Cir. 1996), a school district's hiring procedures were found to be inadequate and the cause of a violation of a student's constitutional rights when she was raped by a school custodian. The school's officials had failed to

investigate criminal records of prospective employees and had employed a school staff of which one-third were convicted criminals.

3. John R. v. Oakland Unified School District, (1989) 48 Cal. 3d 438.

4. Karen Cullen (1995), "Student's rape accusation divides Worcester School," *Boston Globe*, April 16, p. 29, 33, at 29.

5. *Id.*

6. Richard Fossey, "Confidential Settlement Agreements Between School Districts and Teachers Accused of Child Abuse: Issues of Law and Ethics," 63 *Education Law Reporter* 1 (1990).

7. Gonzalez v. Yselta Independent School District, 996 F.2d 745 (5th Cir. 1993).

8. Nan D. Stein (1993), "It Happens Here Too: Sexual Harassment and Child Sexual Abuse in Elementary and Secondary Schools." In S. K. Biklen and D. Pollard (Eds.), *Gender and Education, Ninety-Second Yearbook of the National Society for the Study of Education* (Chicago: University of Chicago Press); Nan D. Stein (1993, December), "Sexual Harassment in Schools, Administrators Must Break the Casual Approach to Objectionable Behavior." *School Administrator*, pp. 14–21.

9. 230 Cal.App. 3d 1349 (1991).

10. Ralph D. Mawdsley, "Compensation for the Sexually Abused Student," 84 *Education Law Reporter* 13, 29 (1993).

11. 766 F. Supp. 1052, 1075 (M.D. Ala. 1990).

12. Alma W. v. Oakland Unified School District, (1981) 123 Cal.App. 3d 133, 141.

13. John R., *supra* note 3, at 451.

14. *Id.*

15. *Id.* at 452.

16. *Id.* at 450.

17. *Id.* at 452.

18. Virgina G. v. ABC Unified School District, (1993) 15 Cal.App. 4th 1848.

11

Do Not Resuscitate Orders: The Psychological Impact of a Do Not Resuscitate Order

Education is a helping profession. As we have discussed throughout this book, educators owe a duty to students. The duty owed, boiled down to its hard shell, is to take reasonable steps to protect students from foreseeable harm. But what happens when the duty to protect is in conflict with the wishes and legal position of the parents and possibly the student?

This situation is occurring within the special education community with heart-rending frequency. Special education students have the right to be educated with their nondisabled peers. This right includes medically fragile children.[1] "Consequently, some children with chronic and terminal conditions are at risk of dying while attending school."[2] One issue associated with this challenge is what duty is owed to those students with foreseeable risks of injury? The second issue may be more difficult for educators to chart a prudent course of action. Generally, we know how to protect students; but with terminally ill students who have a do not resuscitate (DNR) order, do we know how to let them die in our schools? The National School Board Association framed the question this way: "How do you respond to parents who bring school personnel an order to not resuscitate their child in a medical emergency?"[3]

ADVANCE DIRECTIVES

An advance directive informs a physician what kind of care you would like to have if you become unable to make decisions, such as being comatose, regarding your medical treatment. An example of an advance directive is a living will, which comes into effect when you are terminally ill. A durable power of attorney is an advance directive that states whom you have directed to make health care decisions for you. It is activated when you are unable to make medical decisions. The third type of advanced directive is a do not resuscitate order. A DNR order is a statement that cardiopulmonary resuscitation not be performed if your heart stops or you stop breathing.[4] A DNR order does not mean abandonment of all medical treatment. It does not, "of itself, rescind the obligations of the health care team to provide quality care, such as suction, oxygen, and pain medication."[5]

THE SCHOOLS AND DNR ORDERS

Some children come to school with severe medical conditions that require a heightened duty of care. For example, in *Cedar Rapids Community School District v. Garret F.*[6] the U.S. Supreme Court held that the Cedar Rapids Community School District must provide Garret with assistance with urinary bladder catheterization once a day, suctioning of his tracheostomy tube as needed, and, at least once every six hours, ambu bagging. He also needs someone who is familiar with his ventilator in the event there is a malfunction or electrical problem and someone who can perform emergency procedures in the event that he experiences autonomic hyperreflexia. A delay of ten minutes in suctioning the tracheostomy could result in death or further brain damage. Children with other medical conditions that leave them medically fragile include those with muscular dystrophy with cardiac involvement that leaves them at risk for sudden death attributable to arrhythmia with the likelihood of successful resuscitation being small.[7]

Sewall and Balkman note that the confluence of special education rights of inclusion for identified students and medical technological advancements has placed students in schools where DNR orders are brought to schools for implementation.[8] While schools receive DNR orders for medically fragile children, the response from schools has not been consistent. A national sample of school districts found that 80 percent of the respondents did not have policies, regulations, or protocols for dealing with students who had DNR orders. Furthermore, 76 percent stated that they would not honor or were uncertain about honoring DNR orders.[9]

There is no consistent response to DNR orders that principals can rely upon to discharge their duty. Do they stand aside when a student with a DNR order goes into cardiac arrest in the classroom and allow the child to die? Do they honor the order and reduce the suffering that the order sought to attain? "A terminally ill child could be saved by emergency care but left physically or mentally impaired—a greater burden for the family and child."[10] Once the decision is made to honor a DNR order, "you can't undo the decision not to resuscitate."[11] The stakes are unquestionably high, and it is a decision that educators, who dedicate their lives to enriching student lives and futures, do not want to make. However, principals, when faced with a DNR order, must act. Their action must conform to the policies of the

> Children with "Do Not Resuscitate" or "Comfort Care" Orders in the School Setting
> The individualized care plan should include:
>
> a. how the child will be moved to the health room or other designated area if serious distress or death should occur at another location in the school;
> b. what, if any, comfort measures should be given to the child;
> c. protocols for notification of the family; and if the child has died in school;
> d. who will do the pronouncement of death; and how the deceased will be removed from school.
>
> In addition, the plan should also address what will happen if the child is in distress, but does not appear to face an imminent risk of death.[12]

school district. Principals can and should give voice to their moral and ethical views during the formulation of a DNR policy.

Some guidance has been provided in some states regarding DNR orders. For example, the Maryland Office of the Attorney General issued an opinion requiring school districts to accept the DNR order from parents and to comply with its directives.[13] The Massachusetts Department of Education developed a comprehensive statewide approach to DNR orders. The policy requires the development of an individualized care plan that is developed in collaboration with the family, the child's physician, and the school physician.

THE PSYCHOLOGICAL IMPACT OF A DO NOT RESUSCITATE ORDER

David J. Hebert, Ph.D.

I suspect that most principals, teachers, and other school personnel view themselves as problem solvers and advice givers. I also suspect they are accustomed to developing policies to respond to known or anticipated crises. This is certainly an understandable organizational activity, seeking consistency and control over myriad events through a rational approach to problem solving. It also causes me to imagine that some administrators may be uncomfortable with the following discussion concerning their staff responsibility in the event of a DNR order. When dealing with the psychological impact of such an event it is not all that effective to emphasize what should be "done," or what one should "do." A dictum in clinical psychology encourages us to understand that there are a number of emotional crises that cannot be cured—they can only be allowed to occur (e.g., grief). The individuals participating in a DNR scenario cannot be rescued with someone else's beliefs or strategy. I imagine that this flies counter to what many administrators see as their role and function.

Utilizing a question-and-answer format I will attempt to address the conundrum described above. The questions are being addressed to me as a consulting psychologist, and the principal asks:

"Would you elaborate on your example of grief and the process implications that this might have for helping my staff and me deal with this possible crisis?"

If you view the DNR event in terms of what would be the predictable emotional response of individuals who are closely associated with the dying person, I believe it would be an experience of *helplessness*. Educators who have ongoing discussions and interactions with students who have a DNR would probably find themselves describing feelings of *frustration* and possibly feelings of *guilt.* What is important to understand in all of this is that psychotherapists generally believe that frustration and guilt are not feelings but are cognitive elaborations that are actually covering up a basic human emotion, namely *anger.* When someone says to you, "I'm so frustrated," and you help him or her talk about it, anger will be found lurking at another level of awareness. Therefore, opportunities to discuss these so-called feelings of frustration will inevitably lead to expressions of anger. But there is more. It is also commonly understood by clinicians that human beings only utilize anger so that they will not have to deal with the *fear* that is fueling the anger.

As long as individuals believe that they feel frustrated or guilty, they never have to discuss the anger and fear that fuels them. The so-called feelings of guilt come in handy with respect to temporary coping but do little for long-term healing.

"Well, I'm not a therapist or counselor, so just what are you telling me to do?"

There is that "do" that I allude to in my beginning comments, and I certainly understand your need to translate all of this into an action plan. However, one does not have to be a counselor in order to help people prepare for predictable emotional responses to a crisis, nor does one have to be a counselor to provide group opportunities for staff members to discuss the emotional chain of events that I noted above. This is with special reference to discussions that occur prior to an anticipated DNR event. Perhaps I can elaborate on this as I respond to more of your questions.

"Well, I can accept that for now, but I want to know about specific applications. For example, what do I say to the teachers who have this child? Should I try to help them build some distance, or do they need to move closer to the student?"

Well, first of all, knowledge is power, and all school personnel will be helped by an opportunity to discuss the chain of events underlined above. If you mean "Should I encourage the teacher to remain psychologically distant from the student because if a DNR event occurs he or she does not want to be emotionally enmeshed with the student?" the answer is an obvious no. My sense is that any distance that could be created will do little in attempting to deal with the aftereffects of a DNR event. The ostrich approach is a very poor long-term resolution to dealing with intense human emotions. Therefore, I would suggest "moving closer" to the student while developing that professional immunity that all caregivers must have in order to deal with the possible loss of the child, client, or patient. The often-used metaphor is that the helper must get as close to the whirlpool as possible without being drawn into the vortex.

"Outside of the teachers, aides, and the school nurse directly involved with the student, who else do you think I should bring into this circle?" And is it better to keep the circle small or expand it?"

I definitely believe that the school counselor should be involved in the circle. I suspect that counselors in most schools are more informed concerning human emotions, and the need to address "fears," than they are given credit for. Many of the school counselors that I know would be very helpful in helping you deal with this impending crisis, and I would recruit them as coleaders of the circle you are describing. In answer to your follow-up question, I suspect that the professionals noted thus far would serve well as the action team.

"When I have meetings with parents and possibly their physician, is it best that you attend?"

If the question is, "Do I think I would have something to offer in such a meeting?" then the answer is yes. I would not be there to attempt to alter the parents' decision about the DNR; however, I believe that my knowledge with respect to post-traumatic stress syndrome would prove valuable to all concerned. The key in all of this is to not lecture anyone but to have the opportunity to make certain that all individuals are as fully informed as possible concerning psychological implications. I would in particular want to make certain that the parents are fully aware of potential impact of their decision on professional roles in the school and the psychological ethos that will surround the DNR event.

"If the teacher or nurse says that they will not honor the order, do you have suggestions as to how I should talk to them? I can't have them take the law into their own hands."

As you well know, you will want to avoid any heavy-handed responses, such as "I am the boss and you will comply with all of this because after all we have no choice in the matter." Just thinking and planning ahead produces enough emotion with this potential DNR event, so you do not want to have a divided crisis team. I am not sure I have any suggestions for this one other than I would make certain that the team discusses the emotional cycle that I noted in my opening comments, with the hope that all team members will conclude that this may not be what we want but it is the way it is going to be, so let's help each other prepare for the potential event. If in the end you have other school personnel who absolutely will not comply with the DNR order, then I am not sure there is anything you can do.

"Is there any other advice that you can give me?"

I think I have provided a few ideas relative to what I promised in my response to your first question; however, a few general issues deserve further elaboration. First of all, I am reminded that in order to move on from a toxic environment human beings need to experience a sense of completion with respect to these powerful events. Most of us understand that the emphasis on informational preparation is one of the main reducers of anticipatory anxiety. This is why considerable effort is currently placed on making certain surgical patients know as much as possible about what they should expect; it was not always so. Your preparatory efforts, including team discussions surrounding their potential and predictable emotional experience, will go a long way to placing a healing balm on the wounds. In addition, it will be important for your crisis team to have the opportunity to discuss the anger and fear that they will experience in the event of an actual DNR event. All of this will go a long way in helping your staff deal with what will undoubtedly be one of the defining moments in their careers.

Oh, one other thing. Be a good listener. As most of us know, there are only two kinds of people in the world: those who are talking, and those who are getting ready to talk. Nobody listens. It is imperative that we listen.

It is not easy to read policy like the one above, or to talk about the death of one of our students;but the fact that it is hard does not make it any less important. Confronting the reality of DNR orders before they are presented does not make it easier, but it may help to clarify the situation.

In the final analysis, we are talking about "loss" and the "meaning" of the loss to the individuals involved. What is the symbolic meaning of this DNR event to each of the participants? Losses have the capacity to produce harmful consequences because they challenge us with the impossibility of balancing our emotions. Threats and traumas unbalance us and require that we find a way to cope. We can find a way of coping that is indirect and therefore produces residual impairment, or we can become educated concerning potential risk variables and reduce our experience of helplessness. Be reminded that there is a bright light in all of this. It is possible for stressful life events to be, individually and collectively, transformational, and in a paradoxical way they present us with opportunities.

NOTES

1. *See*, Detsel v. Sullivan, 895 F.2d 58 (2d. Cir. 1990).
2. American Academy of Pediatrics, Committee on School Health and Committee on Bioethics, "Do Not Resuscitate Orders in School," 105 *Pediatrics* 878 (April 2000).
3. National School Board Association, "School boards weigh response to do-not-resuscitate orders," *School Board News* 1 (August 23, 2005).
4. American Academy of Family Physicians, "Advance Directives and Do Not Resuscitate Orders." Site visited 12/23/05, http://familydoctor.org/003.xml.
5. American Academy of Pediatrics, *supra* note 2.
6. Cedar Rapids Community School District v. Garret F., 119 S.Ct. 992 (1999).
7. American Academy of Pediatrics, *supra* note 2.
8. Angela Maynard Sewall and Kathy Balkman, "DNR Orders and School Responsibility: New Legal Concerns and Qestions," 23 *Remedial and Special Education* 7 (2002).
9. Michael B. Kimberly, Amanda L. Forte, Jean M. Carroll, and Chris Feudtner, "Pediatric Do-Not-Resuscitate Orders and Public Schools: A National Assessment of Policies and Laws," 5 *American Journal of Bioethics* 59–65 (2005).
10. National School Board Association, *supra* note 3 at 2.
11. *Id.*
12. Anne H. Sheetz, Director of School Health Services, Massachusetts Department of Education, memorandum to school nurses and school physicians (December 3, 2004). Site visited 10/31/05, http://ww.doe.mass.edu/news/news.asp?id=2154.
13. Sewall and Balkman, *supra* note 8 at 9.

12

Safety Plan, Communication, and the Press

This book is predicated on the idea of the principal being proactive and not just reactive. Acting proactively involves planning. Principals need to develop a safety plan and a communication plan in case of crisis or a significant event that raises concerns of parents and the community about how well the school is protecting its students.

SAFETY PLAN

Jointly develop with the faculty, central office, and health services a school safety response plan that is implemented when an accident occurs. Most schools have implemented security plans regarding what to do when the security of the school, student body, and employees are threatened. A safety response plan dovetails into that plan. At a minimum such a plan should address the following (in addition to Christian Keiner's sidebar in chapter 4):

School and Community Services

What nursing/health services are available at school during the week? What backup services are available when onsite services are not provided? Has there been coordination with the local fire services and fire rescue? Has all of the information that they have requested been provided?

Student Medical Conditions

Do you have a readily available list of medically fragile children (children who have severe reactions to peanuts or bee stings, for example)? Is that list provided to faculty and staff when a student on the list goes off campus for a school-sponsored activity? Do you have designated personnel who have been trained in the use of EpiPens to counteract severe allergic reactions? And do you have written permission from the parent or guardian to use the EpiPen, including a statement from the student's physician detailing the conditions under which the EpiPen should be used?

Communications

Procedures for contacting parents of injured children, requesting ambulance services, and notifying the superintendent's office should be put into place. A spokesperson, possibly the principal or district-office-designated media spokesperson must be identified. Written and oral communications must be carefully drafted and delivered for accuracy and tone. Confidentiality must be protected. Most of the time, early release of information concerning potential harm is better than a late communication. Is it clear who is in charge over what activities and who is the backup in case of absence?

First Aid

Who has been trained to give first aid in your building? Do your faculty and staff have an understanding of basic first aid, such as not moving a student/employee who may have sustained a neck, head, or back injury? Do you have readily accessible and currently stocked first aid supplies?

Ethos of Care

Is there a pervasive attitude that your first response and first concern is in aiding the student and not in protecting the school?

COMMUNICATING WITH THE PUBLIC AND THE PRESS

A very good general rule of communication is: more and sooner is better than less and later. It is worth remembering that there are no real secrets in a school. If a problem or crisis has occurred at school that parents and community members are likely to perceive as a threat, the principal must be prepared to talk about it to the extent that it does not violate confidential information that we are legally and ethically bound to protect.

Education World provides some useful information about communicating in a crisis. I have summarized their recommendations below.[1]

- Public relations consultant William Harms states, "Be prepared to tell the facts right away. Don't let things stew and get out of control." Make sure that you understand the circumstances and define the problem. As we have observed in political races and what we know from our study of policy, the definition of a situation or a person helps to define the discussion, the options, and potential solutions.
- Communicate with your faculty and staff first. This keeps them in the loop, builds community, and elicits cooperation.
- Communicate with your parents. Write a clear statement to be sent home with your students on the day the crisis occurs. Be clear and concise, state the facts, and let the parents know that you have a plan. "More information is better—the sketchier the information, the more likely parents will be to fill in the blanks with rumor and speculation."
- Keep outsiders off the school grounds.
- If you think the media may be drawn to the situation, be prepared.
- Refer all media calls to one spokesperson. That person must be prepared with the facts. It is best to have a fact sheet that can be referred to for consistency and accuracy. It is too easy for the emotion of the situation to overwhelm the reason that is necessary.
- "Be honest but don't be lured into speculation. Stick to the facts. If you don't know the answer to a question, admit it and offer to get back to the reporter—and then do so."
- Never tell a reporter something you do not want to see on the front page of your local newspaper or on the evening local news. Consider that nothing is off the record.

- "If you are asked a question that is off point, confused, or inappropriate, answer the question you wish had been asked. What is important here is that . . .' Reporters are often satisfied to receive a clear, quotable statement, even if it is not perfectly responsive."
- Stop talking when you have answered the question or when you have made your statement. Do not feel that you must fill in silences; it is an easy way to say more than you intended. Short responses are often better than long, rambling answers.
- If you are angry or upset, try to postpone the interview.

When faced with a crisis or a threat, consider your options and act decisively to ensure the health and safety of your students, faculty, and staff. People expect principals to be leaders and to act like leaders. A crisis calls for leadership, and if the principal does not exercise it, who will?

NOTE

1. Education World, "The Number One Rule About Communicating in a Crisis?—Communicate in a Crisis!" Site visited 3/2/06, www.education-world.com/a_admin/admin/admin123.shtml#crisis.

13

The Proactive, Prudent Principal

Teachers and principals owe a duty of reasonable care to their students. Teachers and principals can be sued for the breach of that duty that caused the injury. There is no magic formula or incantation that can be invoked that will protect an educator from such lawsuits. The best protection from lawsuits lies within the control of educators—how they consistently discharge their professional duties. Attentiveness to the duty that is owed students is important in that it builds habits of action. Knowledge of our duty is critical. Review of how we discharge our professional duty is imperative.

The prudent principal should consider the following:

1. Insert a section in the staff handbook that describes the responsibilities of staff members concerning appropriate supervision (see appendix B). The section could include comments on the importance of supervision, the educator's legal responsibility to the students, and the need to be diligent in performing supervision. The principal should bring to the attention of the teachers this handbook section at the first faculty meeting. This agenda item should appear in the minutes of the meeting. The principal should contact any personnel who were absent, and the importance of the section should be made clear. The principal should write a notes-to-file memo stating when and with whom he or she met. This documentation demonstrates prudence and reasonableness and

may help to protect the principal from a suit for negligent supervision of the faculty when a student is injured. Often the principal is named as a defendant in a suit for negligence and a paper trail of prudent actions assists his or her defense.

2. While on duty the teacher or aide should be assigned to a specific location. That location should be clearly defined (a map in the handbook is helpful) with enough supervision allotted to dangerous areas. The educator should circulate through the assigned area and report to duty on time.
3. At least twice a year the principal should place a notice in the weekly bulletin to teachers directing them to review the safety rules with their students. The teacher should make a note in his or her lesson plan book as to when the review took place and follow up with any students who were absent.
4. Teachers and other supervisors should be instructed that when supervising students involved in class activities or playground recess, their main job is supervision and instruction, not participation in the activity. Often there is a tendency to play in the game instead of supervising the game. For example, a high school substitute teacher was supervising a boy's physical education class when an overweight (327 pounds) student collapsed and later died of cardiac arrest brought on by heat stroke. The boys played for approximately twenty minutes in a poorly ventilated gym at a temperature of ninety degrees. A Louisiana Court of Appeals upheld a judgment of $560,000 for negligent supervision. The court held that the teacher "participated in the game himself rather than observe and monitor the students as he should have under these conditions."[1] Had the teacher not participated in the game, would he have seen the signs of impending heat stroke?
5. Set up a safety inspection plan with the custodian and keep to the plan. Any potential problem areas must be dealt with immediately and effectively. Either the dangerous condition must be repaired or, barring a time constraint, the area or piece of equipment should be removed from service.
6. Ask teachers to conduct periodic inspections of equipment and areas under their control. If equipment is broken and presents a foreseeable risk of injury, have the educator immediately take it out of service and notify the principal so that repair may be undertaken. While the principal has ultimate responsibility for maintaining a safe environment, the duty owed to students requires that all educators act reasonably to reduce the likelihood

of injury. The responsibility to repair resides with the principal, but all faculty and staff carry the duty to warn students and to take appropriate steps to reduce harm.

7. Permission slips pose a challenge for principals. They may provide a false sense of security. It is prudent to adopt the position that they do not protect us from our negligence. At a minimum, a signed permission slip may indicate that we have permission to transport or remove a student from the normal setting of the school and thus have not kidnapped the student. Its practical value, then, may be more public relations than a statement that we can now disregard the duty that we owe to the students. In fact, the duty may be heightened because of the foreseeablity of additional dangers associated with where the students are going and what they will do once they get there. We require permission slips because the student will not be involved in the normal school routine with its regular practices and protections. A non-routine activity usually requires notice and permission.

Zirkel states that the legal status of permission slips or release forms varies, "but they are generally considered to be neither rock-solid protection nor legally valueless in terms of immunity."[2] However, even if the protection afforded by permission slips is questionable, the prudent principal will strictly adhere to any policy that requires the receipt of permission slips before a student can take place in a school activity either on campus or off campus. To ignore the policy is to place yourself in jeopardy. Not only will you have to defend your probably unprofessional and possibly insubordinate decision, there typically is no upside in allowing a student to participate in the activity. For example, Zirkel notes that a Missouri principal was disciplined for not following board policy requiring teachers to secure written parental permission for field trips.[3]

Boilerplate permission slips must be reviewed periodically. However, permission slips that are used in unusual circumstances, such as an overnight trip, should be reviewed for the individual circumstances of the trip. For example, these are some recommended additions I made to the standard permission slip for a school district that sponsored a field trip to Washington, D.C., for eighth graders:

> We must stress that the school district cannot ensure the safety of our students. Our obligation is to take reasonable precautions in light of foreseeable dangers. Your child also has a responsibility for his/her safety

and the safety of others. Because Washington, D.C., may be a new experience for your child, it is imperative that your son/daughter obey all rules and directives of the chaperones and, most important, not wander away from the group at any time.

I understand that no medical services or medical personnel will be provided by the school district for this educational field trip. I will provide the school staff with medical or other important information that I believe the school should know about my child. Every effort will be made to keep the provided information confidential.

_____I am not attaching any medical or other information regarding my child.

_____I am attaching information on my child's emergency medical or important other needs. I have attached verification from my physician and directions for any necessary and vital prescription medication that my child must take.

Below is a sample of a portion of Portsmouth (New Hampshire) High School's student permission form used when students leave the campus for school-sponsored activities.

In case of medical emergency, in the event that I/we cannot be reached, I/we authorize a representative of the school department to procure and consent to any medical examination, diagnostic process, or course of treatment, including transportation and hospital care, to be rendered to my/our child by or under the supervision of any duly licensed health care provider. A copy of this authorization is to be accepted as valid as the original. I/We understand that the information herein may be necessary by the school department.

Signature: Parent/Guardian Date:

I/We understand that the school department does not provide personal or health insurance coverage for students.

In arranging transportation or medical treatment in an emergency, the school department does not assume financial liability for the student's medical care.

I/We understand that the information provided herein may be used as necessary by the school department.

Signature: Parent/Guardian Date:

8. Make a copy of the site plan for your school. Each time an injury occurs mark the spot of the injury on the site plan. You can color code it for the time of day and type of incident if you choose.

The major use of the plotting is to ascertain the dangerous spots at your school. You can then use the data to make corrections to practices and policies, as well as to discuss liability issues with the faculty and staff. I have also used this type of data plotting for discipline problems. Through its use we were able to find holes in our supervision. It is quite clear that if the adults in the school don't own specific areas of the school through enforcement and presence, the students will. And the students who claim the territory don't usually do so for benign reasons.

For example, I was giving a presentation to the faculty in a semiurban school district when a teacher told of a problem in the hallways of one of their high schools. She stated that the students created a gauntlet in certain areas that some students were afraid to traverse, opting instead to take a circuitous route to their classroom. She asked my advice because the inservice was on sexual harassment.

I first asked, semirhetorically, Where are the adults? If there is no adult presence or a limited adult presence in that hallway, then some of the students have claimed it as their territory.

I recommended that during the passing time all teachers who were not legitimately engaged in a more compelling act than making the hallways safe for students should step outside their doorway for the first minute or two of the passing period. This would create a phalanx of teachers and adults in that hallway. This would likely deter most behavior, and that behavior that is not deterred can then be appropriately addressed.

I explained to the teachers that one spring when I was a principal in southern California I was having a problem with an increase of student fights right after school let out for the day. Not only did we contact the parents about the problem, but all of the faculty and staff stepped outside their classroom doors (we did not have interior corridors at the school) for the first several minutes to let students know that they were being supervised. The incidents of fighting soon dropped, and we withdrew the extra supervision. The problem was seen as a school problem in which all adults had a responsibility. It was not phrased or viewed: if it is not my students then it is not my problem. This leads to my last recommendation, one of symbols rather than law.

9. I strongly believe that all educators at a school have a responsibility for all students. When I was a principal I consistently

You took this quiz at the end of chapter 2. Please take it again at this time. You can compare your scores for changes and then check your pre- and post-test scores with the answers in Appendix H.

POST-TEST ON TORT LIABILITY

TRUE or FALSE

1. T F Educators owe a legal duty to their students.
2. T F The reasonable person concept applies to ed ucators under tort liability/negligence.
3. T F Principals cannot be held liable when a teacher's act or failure to act causes an injury.
4. T F Proximate cause is a defense in tort liability/negligence cases.
5. T F As the foreseeability of injury increases so must the duty owed increase.
6. T F Breach of duty is an aspect of the prima facie case in tort liability issues.
7. T F Sufficient injury or actual loss or injury must be proved in tort liability/negligence cases.
8. T F Adequate/proper supervision is an aspect of the duty eductors owe their students.
9. T F All torts involve negligence.

discussed this viewpoint with the faculty and staff. I asserted that our school was not an egg crate in which each classroom was walled off and protected from the next. Our classes were not meant to separate us as unconnected entities. We were responsible for the school and all of the students in the school and not for those students in our individual classes. We worked on establishing a strong ethic that we were the true architects and builders of the school.[4] We were responsible for what the school was and what it could become.

We decide through the small daily decisions that we make and the large policies that we adopt not only what we value but

> who we value. We are responsible for building the school, not with brick and mortar, but with the infusion of enduring values that define who we are as educators and what is the core of our school.

The principal, faculty, and staff who genuinely believe that they are part of something bigger than just the dukedom of their classroom avoid liability not just because liability is costly but because it is the right thing to do. In schools where all students are valued, students are better protected.

When a principal is in court defending against a suit for negligence, what that principal has done prior to the injury to inform and supervise faculty activity is critical to the defense. The principal who takes reasonable steps to inform his or her faculty of their legal responsibility to students and then supervises the discharge of that responsibility goes a long way in protecting her- or himself as well as students, faculty, staff, and the school district. All too often the discussion about legal responsibility takes place after the injury has occurred and facts cannot be changed.

The discussion about our legal responsibility should be part of an ongoing schoolwide dialogue. Professional practice includes reasonably discharging our legal responsibilities. Building habits of mind about our duty builds habits of action.

NOTES

1. James v. Jackson, 898 So.2d 596, 599 (La.App. 4 Cir. 2005).
2. Perry A. Zirkel, "Permission Forms," 84 *Principal*, 8 (January–February 2005).
3. Bell v. Board of Education of St. Louis, 711 S.W.2d 950 (Mo. Ct.App. 1986).
4. When I was the chair of the Department of Education at the University of New Hampshire, a large and complex department for which it seemed like I was a principal once again, we used the aphorism "Hammers and Rulers—We Build What We Value" to frame a core understanding of our responsibility. One of the things that we valued was the people in our department. Each faculty agenda had a section under the heading of "Hammers and Rulers—We Build What We Value" called "Supporting Our Own." In this section we listed professional and personal accomplishments and successes. Our belief was that if we didn't support and celebrate our own, perhaps no one else would.

V

APPENDIXES

V

APPENDIXES

Appendix A

Case Studies Revisited

In addition to discussing the Guiding Questions, the four-part prima facie case of duty owed, breach, causation, and sufficient injury can be applied to the three case studies from chapter 3.

RECESS DUTY AT THE SWINGS

1. *Would a reasonable teacher go to the lounge for a cup of coffee instead of going directly to the assigned duty?*

A reasonable person would go directly to the assigned duty station. This conclusion is quite apparent, especially with the knowledge of the injury that occurred at the duty station. The less straightforward issue is when a teacher is delayed while attending to another matter associated with his or her duties. For example, a teacher stays behind to attend to another student, or the teacher has to use the bathroom. The reasons for being late may well be legitimate. But the courts, and especially a jury, will view the situation with perfect hindsight. The courts will want to know for what purpose and for how long the teacher was absent from the duty. Did the teacher try to make arrangements for coverage when the time away became unreasonable? Are there procedures in place for these eventualities?

2. *Would Mr. Roberts's duty increase if the teachers had specific knowledge that the injured student had a propensity to climb the swing set?*

Yes. Knowledge of a hazardous situation requires a reasonable response. Either the student should be removed from the area or heightened supervision of the student must be provided.

3. *If there is another teacher on duty and that teacher notices that Mr. Roberts is not on duty, has the duty of that teacher increased to encompass the swing set?*

More than likely the answer is yes. A teacher may have a specific assignment, but if she or he has knowledge of a potentially dangerous situation and the teacher takes no action to reduce the likelihood of injury, the teacher probably has not acted as a reasonable teacher discharging the duty of adequate supervision. One of the problems that occurs when a teacher is habitually late for a duty is that another teacher who is on duty may have his or her duty expanded to take up the slack.

4. *If the principal knows that Mr. Roberts has the history stated above, can the principal be liable for negligent supervision if he or she does not take appropriate steps regarding Mr. Roberts?*

Principals, as well as teachers, must act as a reasonable prudent person would under the same or similar circumstances. They owe the same duty of care to students that teachers owe. A reasonable principal would take action in light of actual knowledge that a teacher was creating an unreasonable risk of harm by failing to consistently attend to his duty on time. The prudent principal periodically checks to make sure that the duties are being covered in a timely and reasonable fashion. Noting on the calendar when these checks are made is a good way to document this reasonable supervision.

A FIELD TRIP TO THE SEASHORE

1. *What steps should the principal have taken regarding the field trip to the seashore?*

Before allowing the students to depart for the trip she should have made sure that all of the students had permission slips to attend the field trip. While the permission slip is generally not a waiver of liability, it does help to establish that the principal follows the policies. However, a principal should not, under any circumstances, let a student attend a field trip away from school without a signed permission slip. Verbal assurances over the phone that a child can attend or take part in the activity can be quickly forgotten if the child is injured. Second, the principal should have reviewed the decision to allow the field trip to take place with only one fully credentialed teacher and one new student teacher. Given the potential dangers associated with the seashore, two adults, only one of whom is a fully credentialed teacher, may be too few. Third, the principal should have reviewed safety rules that the teacher would use for the field trip.

2. *What steps should the teacher have taken while on the bus and after letting the students off the bus?*

The directions to the students should have been clearer about what was meant by being careful. There should have been a check for understanding regarding the rules. The large group of students should have been broken up into two smaller groups with an adult assigned to each. The adults should have made periodic checks by doing a quick head count of each group. The adults were notified by the antics of the two boys that they were not attentive to the field trip. This should have triggered heightened supervision of the two.

3. *How did the seashore increase the duty owed to the students?*

The seashore is not the normal classroom. The foreseeability of injury, particularly of drowning, is evident. The outcroppings provided places where the students would be out of sight and thus unsupervised. Heightened supervision was called for because of the foreseeability of injury.

4. *How is time important to this case study?*

The students were showing off for fifteen minutes. A reasonable teacher would have intervened and increased scrutiny of the students. This time lag could indicate inattentiveness to the duty of adequately supervising the students. A second issue is the forty-five minutes the students were missing. This is entirely too long for two students to drop out of sight. Once again, would a reasonable teacher allow forty-five minutes to pass in an area of increased risk without knowing the whereabouts and activities of the two students?

MS. SMITH'S VERY BAD DAY

1. Did Ms. Smith owe an increased duty to Steve?

Yes. Ms. Smith had actual knowledge that Steve often did not put on his goggles and would take them off when he needed to keep them on. This knowledge increased the foreseeability specific to Steve that he engaged in risky behavior. While Ms. Smith does not insure Steve's safety, she must respond reasonably by adjusting the duty owed to Steve in light of this knowledge.

2. Was Steve's injury foreseeable?

Yes. It was foreseeable that if the students did not wear goggles for the experiment they could be injured by the caustic chemicals. Furthermore, since Ms. Smith knew that Steve often did not wear his goggles, she had knowledge of his dangerous propensity, thus requiring greater supervision of Steve.

3. Would Ms. Smith be liable if she had instructed the students to wear their goggles and after she checked and turned away from Steve he took his goggles off and immediately got the caustic chemicals in his eyes?

No. If Ms. Smith had checked to make sure that the students had on their goggles and if she had specifically checked Steve because of his known aversion to wearing the goggles and then Steve whipped off the goggles, the courts would most likely consider this to be a spontaneous act. But, if Steve had removed the goggles for five or ten minutes before being injured the court would probably question whether a reasonable and prudent chemistry teacher during an experiment using caustic chemicals would not have seen Steve's dangerous act.

4. The textbook provides a warning about wearing goggles. Is that sufficient to relieve Ms. Smith of liability?

Probably not. It is more prudent to warn students and then to check to make sure that they have complied. Ms. Smith did neither. We should not be willing to leave this potentially dangerous situation and our professional reputations to a defense that says that the students should have known and that the injured student contributed to his or her injury. I believe that it is prudent to warn students of known dangers and then take reasonable steps to reduce the likelihood of injury.

Appendix B

Handbook Policy on Supervision

It is well established that the proper supervision of students is an important professional and legal responsibility. We owe our students a duty of providing reasonable care. An orderly and safe environment is necessary for the delivery of quality education. Therefore, at ____________________ school, all educators owe all students four obligations.

ADEQUATE SUPERVISION

- Report to all duty assignments on time (see map for assigned duty areas).
- Circulate through your duty area and your classroom, paying particular attention to areas and activities that pose an increased risk of injury.
- Be vigilant while supervising students. If you are on recess duty, your responsibility is to supervise all of the students in your assigned area. Your attention must be focused on the supervision. Supervision is not a time to play games or engage in other activities with the students.
- If you know that a particular student has a propensity to act dangerously in a specific manner, your supervision of that student must increase with the known risk of injury.

- The greater the foreseeable risk of injury to students, the greater our duty to increase the vigilance of our supervision.

PROPER INSTRUCTIONS

- Proper instructions are necessary to reduce the risk of injury when students undertake an activity, especially an activity that has an increased risk of harm to students.
- Repeat the instructions on how to complete a task that has a heightened risk of danger as often as needed. Do not assume because students heard the directions once that they will be remembered.
- When you go over safety rules with students, note it in your lesson plan book.
- Review playground and classroom safety rules at least once each semester and note when you do it in your lesson plan book. Also, if any students are absent when you review the rules, contact the students to review the same information and also note that contact in your lesson plan book.

PROPER MAINTENANCE OF BUILDINGS, GROUNDS, AND EQUIPMENT

- Conduct periodic inspections of equipment under your control. If equipment is broken or presents a foreseeable risk of injury, immediately take it out of service and notify the office so those repairs may be undertaken.
- Provide warnings regarding known or reasonably foreseeable hazards.
- If you have knowledge of a hazard that can likely cause injury, you must take steps to reduce the risk of injury.

How we conduct our professional duties is important. Attentiveness to the duty that we owe our students is critical.

I am the decisive element in the classroom. It is my personal approach that creates the climate. It is my daily mood that makes the weather. As a teacher I possess tremendous power to make a child's life miserable or joyous. I can be a tool of torture or an instrument of inspiration. I can humiliate or humor, hurt or heal. In all situations it is my response that decides whether a crisis will be escalated or de-escalated, and a child humanized or de-humanized. (Hiam G. Ginott, Teacher & Child, 1972)

Appendix C

Tort Liability Handout

PRIMA FACIE CASE FOR NEGLIGENCE

Duty Owed

- Educators owe students a duty to anticipate foreseeable dangers and take necessary precautions to protect students entrusted in their care from such dangers.

BREACH OF DUTY

- Did the educator's action, or failure to act, create an unnecessary risk of harm? This standard of care is measured against a reasonable person (teacher) standard: did the teacher act as a reasonable and prudent teacher would have acted in the same or similar circumstances? Did the educator fail to exercise an appropriate standard of care (duty owed) given the age of the students, the environment, and the type of instructional activity?

CAUSATION

Cause-in-Fact

- Is there a causal or sequential connection between the teacher's action or inaction and the resultant injury? This is the but-for test.

Proximate Cause

- Was it foreseeable that the teacher's action or inaction would cause the injury? Was the injured person a foreseeable plaintiff?

SUFFICIENT INJURY

- The plaintiff must have sustained a sufficient injury in order for the court to provide a remedy.

Obligations of an Educator

Provide Adequate Supervision
Provide Adequate Instructions
Provide Properly Maintained Equipment
Provide Warnings Regarding Known Hazards

Appendix D

Liability and the Science Lab

HANDOUT FOR SCIENCE TEACHERS

The science lab may well be the most dangerous place in our school. The need to provide hands-on learning activities often creates heightened danger for some of our lessons. Therefore, extra planning and constant vigilance is required in order to provide safe instruction.

The Council of State Science Supervisors has developed a list of duties that form the basis of the duty that we owe our students at __________ school. In addition, working safely is an expectation and a condition of employment.

Duty of Instruction

- Instruction given prior to beginning a laboratory activity should
  - be accurate;
  - be appropriate to the situation;
  - address reasonably foreseeable dangers;
  - identify and clarify any specific risk involved;
  - explain proper procedures to be used; and
  - present comments concerning appropriate and inappropriate conduct in the lab.

- Instruction must follow professional and district guidelines.
- Develop proper safety guidelines, inform and instruct students on those guidelines, and require that those guidelines be implemented. Do not allow students to conduct experiments until they have passed a test on appropriate safety rules. Keep a copy of the passed tests for your records.
- Remember, "teachers who set bad examples by not following proper laboratory procedures may be sued if injury results from students following the teacher's bad example."[1]

Duty of Supervision

- Misbehavior of any type must not be tolerated.
- The greater the degree of danger, the higher the level of supervision required of the teacher.
- Younger students and students with disabilities who may not fully understand the dangers of the instructional activity require heightened supervision.
- Be sure to circulate through the lab when an instructional activity is taking place.
- Even if you have warned students about the dangers of the activity, such as the necessity to wear protective eye goggles, a number of times, do it again when the risk of danger is foreseeable. Don't just tell students to put on their goggles; instead, watch to make sure that all students have them on before you allow them to start the exercise.
- If in doubt about the ability of providing a reasonably safe environment for an activity, do not perform the activity and report the safety concern as soon as possible to the proper individual.

Duty of Maintenance of Equipment

- Never use defective equipment for any reason.
- Establish regular inspection schedules and procedures for checking safety and first aid equipment. Document these inspections.
- Follow all safety guidelines concerning proper labeling, storage, and disposal of chemicals.
- File written reports with the administration for maintenance and correction of hazardous conditions or defective equipment.

Maintaining Safe Facilities

- Keep class enrollments to the recommended safety level for the square footage of the laboratory.
- Use safety shields, especially when performing demonstration experiments in an open area.[2]
- Secure chemical storage separate from laboratory, classroom, and prep/equipment storeroom.
- Provide minimum ventilation with nonrecirculated air.
- Provide appropriate eyewash and safety shower.[3]

NOTES

1. Council of State Science Supervisors. Site visited 10/16/04, http://css.enc.org/media/scisafe.pdf.

2. A chemistry teacher conducted an experiment involving igniting various metal chloride salts. When the teacher poured methanol into the final metal chloride salt a fireball flashed across his desk, engulfing students sitting across from him. The fire ignited vapors in the room. No shield was used between the flammable material and the student observers. David J. Hoff (April 20, 2003), "Science-lab Safety Upgraded After Mishaps," *Education Week*. Site visited 3/17/05, http://www.edweek.org/ew/ew_printstory.cfm?slug=33labsafety.h22.

3. *See*, Sandra S. West, Julie F. Westerlund, Amanda L. Stephenson, Nancy C. Nelson, and Cynthia K. Nyland, "Safety in Science Classrooms: What Research and Best Practices Say," *The Educational Forum*, 174–183 (2003).

Appendix E1

Tort Scenarios

HANDOUT FOR INSERVICE

Please read the following scenarios based on court cases. They will form the basis for discussion. If you found the educator liable, what reasonable steps would you recommend that the educator should have taken to protect students?

A. At the beginning of a chemistry course, the instructor gave an orientation and safety lecture as well as distributing a handout summarizing laboratory procedures and safety instructions. The assigned reading in the textbook included a warning not to use a flammable liquid near a flame. These instructions and precautions were not repeated. More than halfway through the semester, Yvonne La Voie, a student in the class, was involved in a class chemistry experiment. The experiment involved separating various chemicals from a mixture by the use of ether as a solvent. After heating the mixture with a Bunsen burner, Yvonne brought a flask of ether back to her laboratory table from the vent hood where it was stored. She poured some of the ether into a funnel and set the flask containing the ether on her lab table, about two and one-half feet from a lighted Bunsen burner. Within seconds, fumes from the ether flask caught on fire, burning Yvonne on her face and chest. Yvonne sued for negligence. Was the instructor negligent?

B. A first-grade student started to sit down on her chair when another student seated next to her quickly pulled out the chair, causing an injury to her tailbone when she hit the floor. The teacher was in front of the class facing the students giving directions. There had been no previous problems with the student who pulled the chair.

   Is the teacher liable?

C. A middle school metal shop teacher took his class outside for a discussion. George, one of the students in the class, picked up a triangular piece of sheet metal from a bench on his way out of the classroom. The teacher arranged the class in a semicircle on the grass. While the teacher talked in front of the class, George threw the piece of sheet metal into the grass. This went on for approximately ten minutes before the piece of metal struck a rock, bounced, and hit another student in the eye.

   Is the teacher liable for the injury?

D. A very large male nonstudent intruder entered a classroom and attacked a male student in the classroom. The female teacher was petite, and after telling the intruder to leave she immediately left the classroom to summon the vice principal, whose office was just down the hall. The injured student sued the teacher for negligence.

   Did the teacher act reasonably in leaving the classroom to summon help?

E. School had been dismissed for fifteen minutes when a group of students started throwing eggs at another student waiting for a public bus at a nearby bus stop. The student ran from the bus stop out into the street, where a vehicle struck him. The student sued the school district for the injuries he sustained.

   Is the school district liable for the off-school premises injury?

Appendix E2

Discussion of Tort Scenarios

A. The issue revolves around two obligations of educators—adequate supervision and proper instructions. First, the assignment involves an increased risk of harm because of a flammable liquid used in proximity to an open flame. This assignment increases the duty owed to the students. Questions to ask regarding supervision include: Was the teacher adequately supervising the chemistry experiment? Did he or she observe the students as they worked with the flammable liquid and the Bunsen burner? Was the teacher circulating through the room, or was she or he seated at the teacher's desk? Questions regarding proper instructions: Did the teacher give any instructions prior to the students starting an assignment with increased risk of harm? Did the teacher intervene at any point with any of the students who had their ether flasks too close to the flame? Given the facts presented, the teacher did not adequately supervise, nor did he or she give proper instructions involving a flammable liquid and an open flame. He or she breached the increased duty owed to Yvonne by failure to adequately supervise the class during an assignment with increased risk of injury and by failure to give proper instructions about the safe handling of the liquid.

B. The major obligation at the center of this issue is adequate supervision. While educators have a duty to supervise students, they are not insurers of children's safety. There is no foreseeability for the unanticipated acts of students. Educators are not liable for "every thoughtless or careless act by which one pupil may injure another."[1] If the event is not foreseeable, then the educator cannot be the cause of the injury. However, the situation changes if the teacher knows that the student in question has a history of this type of behavior and the teacher does not increase the vigilance of supervision for this student.

C. The major question is whether or not the educator's supervision was adequate. The student threw the metal shard into the grass for ten minutes prior to the injury. This activity was not just foreseeable, it was seen, or should have been seen. There was enough notice of the activity that a reasonably prudent educator would have seen the action and taken reasonable steps to stop the dangerous activity.

D. The teacher is required to act as a reasonable and prudent person would act under the same or similar circumstances. The reasonable person has the same physical characteristics as the defendant teacher, in this case a smaller than average height and weight. Because of the size difference and the refusal to stop the attack when directed, the reasonable course of action was to get help, which could aid the student. The teacher acted in a reasonable manner.

E. Generally, a school's duty to adequately supervise a student ends when it relinquishes physical custody and control of the student.[2] The school did not owe a duty because the student had been safely dismissed from the school premises approximately fifteen minutes before the accident, which occurred beyond the boundaries of the school property. Also, there was no indication that the school officials had any notice of impending or imminent harm to the student.

NOTE

1. Danna v. Sewanhaka Cent. Sch. Dist., 662 N.Y.S.2d 71 (A.D. Dept. 1997).

2. See, Bowers v. Board of Education, 742 N.Y.S.2d 659, 660 (A.D. 2 Dept. 2002).

Appendix F

Local Legal Issue: Their Cup Runneth Over

Sherry Belcher, M.Ed.

In my school law class, I require the students to write a local legal issue case study. This requirement gives the students the opportunity to apply legal principles to a legal issue that has arisen in their school or school district. The requirements for the assignment are stated below.

- Discuss the facts of a legal issue that has arisen in your work setting.
- Please feel free to disguise the school district, school, and participants.
- Your case study will not be shared without your prior permission.
- After establishing the pertinent facts, complete an IRAC (Issue, Rule, Analysis, Conclusion) on the fact pattern.
- Finish the case study by analyzing the action that was taken. If the issue has not yet been resolved, discuss how you would resolve it.

The following is a sample of a case study on a legal issue. It can be used for discussion purposes or it can be used as an example of how to write a legal issue case study. Permission to use this paper was given by the student author. I appreciate Ms. Belcher's willingness to share her work.

THEIR CUP RUNNETH OVER

C. C. Beaker, a veteran teacher with ten years' experience teaching high school science, was in his second year at Retexe High School teaching chemistry to 100- (honors) and 200-level classes. He had not had any discipline problems or parent complaints at Retexe. It was March, and the end of the school year was in sight. There had been no accidents or injuries of any kind prior to March 30, 2005, when a gas release occurred in lab 232, affecting several students (Bailey 2005).

Retexe High School has an established protocol in science labs that must be followed before each and every experiment. That protocol consists of the following:

- the lab must come from a legitimate source (an institute of some type)
- the lab needs to be in a written format for students
- Materials Safety and Data Sheet (MSDS) must be read orally by the teacher so that students understand hazards of chemicals. The MSDS covers:
  - flammability, exposure, reactivity of chemicals being used
  - use of protective gear
  - effects of chemicals: short term (acute), long term (chronic), and lethal dose (50 percent)
  - first aid protocol and emergency procedures

Mr. Beaker's lab investigated the properties of oxygen gas. This lab was from the supplemental material accompanying the textbook and had been used by other instructors. After being informed that the chemical supply room did not have the necessary amount of hydrogen peroxide to conduct the oxygen preparation lab, Mr. Beaker decided to use an alternate method that he had used several times previously while working in another school. This second method involved the decomposition of a sodium hypochlorite solution (household bleach) by using cobalt II chloride as a catalyst. After searching the Internet, an official procedure involving this reaction was found on the Woodrow Wilson Fellowship website (www.woodrow.org/teachers/chemistry/institutes/1986/exp7/html).

This new lab was identical to the hydrogen peroxide procedure he had intended on using, except for the preparation of oxygen. The new lab called for the students to collect gas in an inverted graduated cylinder so that they could calculate a theoretical concentration of bleach while correcting for the classroom pressure and temperature. This would allow students to make the connection between the gas laws and the current topic in the classroom.

Mr. Beaker prudently conducted a dry run of the lab on March 29 to be sure the reaction could be run safely in the classroom. The run was successful but for one problem. While collecting gas in a graduated cylinder, the 150 ml of bleach required emptied the cylinder, destroying the purpose of the experiment. Mr. Beaker decided to reduce the amount of bleach to 80 ml.

A second dry run was conducted the next day (March 30) during first period, his free period, the concern being that the amount of bleach being used with the graduated cylinder would still be in excess, causing the reading to go off scale. After running the experiment for a second time, Mr. Beaker decided to further reduce the amount of bleach to 20 ml for the graduated cylinder. Per science protocol, Mr. Beaker conferred with the science safety director, Mr. Ian Goggles, regarding his amended lab. Mr. Goggles voiced concern regarding the use of bleach in the experiment instead of the required hydrogen peroxide. They both consulted a chemical manual on the reactivity of sodium hypochlorite and, noting there was no reference to this reaction in particular, went back to the MSDS sheets. The MSDS sheets listed only a warning pertaining to mixing bleach with ammonia compounds.

Mr. Beaker's third-period class arrived, a homogeneous mix of twenty-four junior boys and girls. Students conduct the labs in pairs spread out over six lab benches. The science wing is the newest addition to the building and therefore was built to safety standards. The lab sheets for the experiment were handed out and Mr. Beaker proceeded to go through the purpose and methodology of the experiment. A summary of the MSDS information was distributed and then read to the class, citing bleach as an irritant when inhaled and cobalt chloride as being moderately toxic. Mr. Beaker ended as he typically did by stressing the need for goggles and aprons. The procedure was then pantomimed by Mr. Beaker as a way of review. It was at this time the class was informed to reduce the amount of bleach being used for the graduated cylinder to 20 ml instead of the 80 ml as indicated by the lab handout.

The students broke off into their pairs, donning protective eye gear and aprons over Mr. Beaker's watchful eyes. They started the experiment, going through the first oxygen collection. Mr. Beaker continually circulated through the room answering questions and constantly checking for safety. One group was having trouble with their oxygen collection so Mr. Beaker went over to them to see what the problem was. While he was there, a student at another bench on the far side of the room, Petri Dish, asked if the amount of bleach indicated on the lab was the correct amount to use. Mr. Beaker, preoccupied with the group he was with and not paying full attention to Petri, answered affirmatively that it was the correct volume of bleach to use. Petri continued with his measuring.

Soon after, a cry of alarm was heard. Looking in the direction of the disturbance, Mr. Beaker noticed the cork was no longer in the flask and a black material (cobalt II and chloride/bleach mixture) was coming out of the top. Petri was exiting the room while other students were standing back away from the eruption. A strong smell of bleach was evident. Mr. Beaker went immediately over to the group where Diane Sect informed him that she and Petri had inhaled some of the gas. Mr. Beaker directed Di to go out into the hallway and get some air with Petri.

Another female from a lab group close by said she felt slightly ill but added that she had felt ill prior to class. Mr. Beaker wrote her a pass and sent her to the nurses' office, escorted by another student. Mr. Beaker then went out into the hall to check on Petri and Di. Di indicted to him that she felt slightly nauseous but otherwise fine and that Petri was in the bathroom. Mr. Beaker went immediately to the boys' bathroom where he found Petri coughing and spitting into the sink to get the taste out of his mouth and sweating profusely. Mr. Beaker asked a teacher next door to watch his class while he escorted Petri and Di to the nurses' station.

On arrival at the nurses' office, Mr. Beaker briefed the nurses of the situation and returned to his room to retrieve the MSDS sheets. While there, he moved his students to the adjacent classroom to be supervised by another teacher and returned to the nurses' office. In the nurses' office, Petri was having extreme respiratory problems and, thus, the nurses told him to stick his head out the window for fresh air while they called poison control. Poison control recommended that 911 be called immediately so that Petri could be transported to the hospital. As is standard procedure, the fire department arrived with the rescue squad.

While the EMTs were tending to Petri, one of the firemen went upstairs to check the classroom in question. Upon arrival in the room, he determined that it was not just a matter of inhaling a gas but rather a "chemical spill." The fireman immediately pulled the closest fire alarm. Students and faculty were quickly evacuated to a building next door used by the high school. While in that building, any students who were in the classroom at the time of the chemical spill were called to the office, where they were checked out by an EMT. After approximately thirty minutes it was determined that the school building would not be able to be secured in a timely manner and, therefore, everyone was sent home.

As it turned out, within sixty minutes the building was secured and any teachers that were still hanging around were allowed back in. Nine students in all were transported to the local hospital. A spokesman for the hospital said the students appeared to be suffering from scratchy throats, slight coughs, mild nausea, headaches, and respiratory problems. He explained that they were not "treated," just observed. He went on further to state that they were instructed to follow up with their family physicians and if anything changed to go immediately to the emergency room. The hospital staff expected the symptoms to clear up within a few days. There was no legal action taken against C. C. Beaker, I. Goggles, Mr. Hide (the principal), or the school district. Students in the classroom drafted and signed a document stating that the accident was not Mr. Beaker's fault. They stated that the student was at fault in measuring the appropriate, or rather inappropriate, amount of bleach.

INTRODUCTION

"School districts have become increasingly concerned about legal liability resulting from student injury" (Lane et al., 340). Considering the number of suits filed each year and the size of the awards, schools have good reason to be alarmed. Tort law offers civil rather than criminal remedies to individuals who are harmed by the unreasonable conduct of others (Cambron-McCabe et al., 468). There are three major categories of school torts: negligence, intentional torts, and defamation (Cambron-McCabe et al., 468). Most tort claims in schools involve negligence.

The preceding case study involves a question of negligence and occurred in the spring of 2005 at a local high school. Interviews were conducted of the teacher involved, school nurses, assistant principal, resource officer, and science department safety personnel. The principal involved at the time, Mr. Hide, has retired. The names have been changed to protect the innocent . . . and the liable.

ISSUE AND RULE

Issue

Was Mr. Beaker negligent and thus liable for the students' injuries?

Rule

Negligence is defined as a "breach of one's legal duty to protect others from unreasonable risks of harm" (Cambron-McCabe et al., 468). There are four elements that must be established for the plaintiffs to prove negligence. The plaintiffs must show: (1) a duty was owed by the defendant to the plaintiffs; (2) the duty was breached by the defendant by a failure to exercise an appropriate standard of care; (3) the negligent conduct was the actual and proximate cause of the plaintiffs' injury; and (4) an actual injury or damage occurred (Cambron-McCabe et al., 468).

ANALYSIS

Was there a duty owed the plaintiffs?

All teachers owe a duty to their students. Essentially, teachers take the place of parents or guardians and therefore must exercise the same reasonable care that a parent or guardian would over their child. Teachers have a common law duty to anticipate foreseeable dangers and take necessary precautions to protect students in their care by:

- providing adequate supervision
- giving proper instruction
- warning students of known dangers
- maintaining equipment, facilities, and grounds

Adequate supervision is determined by the circumstances that surround the situation, such as age of students and type of classroom. In the case before us, a high school chemistry lab was being conducted with toxic chemicals being used and reactions between them expected; therefore, Mr. Beaker had a heightened responsibility for adequate supervision, proper instruction, and warning students of known dangers. The greater the risk for harm, the greater the need for instruction.

> Proper supervision is particularly important in settings that pose significant risks to students, such as . . . science laboratories, and school grounds where known dangers exist. In these settings, it is critical that school personnel provide both proper instruction and adequate supervision to reduce the likelihood of injury to children and staff. (Cambron-McCabe et al., 469)

Mr. Beaker demonstrated adequate supervision by circulating around the room observing and watching students as they performed their lab. Proper warnings were administered to students via the MSDS sheets that were read aloud and from his pantomiming of the methodology of the lab to be done. Mr. Beaker did two dry runs of the experiment after he realized he had to make a substitution, thereby helping him foresee any problems that might occur. He also verified his replacement of hydrogen peroxide with bleach with the science department safety personnel. He appeared to be cautious, careful, and thoughtful in his approach to the lab and met his duty to provide adequate supervision and proper warning to his students. The duty owed of maintaining the equipment, facilities, and grounds is not an issue in this case.

The one critical element that Mr. Beaker failed to meet is proper instruction. Mr. Beaker decided after doing a dry run during the first period of the day to lower the amount of bleach even more from his original decision, finalizing an amount of 20 ml instead of 80 ml. When his third-period class arrived he *told them* to use 20 ml of bleach instead of 80 ml *as noted* in the lab. By not giving students a revised handout or, at the very least, making sure that each and every student changed their copy to read 20 ml immediately after he gave the correction, he set himself and students up for a possible mishap. "Following such instruction, effort should be made to determine whether the material was heard and understood" (Cambron-McCabe et al., 473). As is kid fashion, Petri either forgot or wanted to verify what the instructions were and asked Mr. Beaker for clarification. At the time Mr. Beaker was preoccupied with another group and misunderstood Petri's question. He thought Petri was asking if the amount of 20 ml was correct when he was actually asking if the amount on the written lab was correct. When Mr. Beaker answered Petri affirmatively, Petri proceeded. By adding over four times the amount of catalyst in the lab he virtually increased the reaction rate exponentially. Mr. Beaker should not have assumed that when he told the students to change the amount of bleach to be used they would remember these verbal instructions when they got to that point in the lab. Consequently, Mr. Beaker failed to give proper instruction to his students before they began their lab by not making sure they corrected their handout.

Was that duty breached by the defendant?

Once it has been established that there is a duty owed the plaintiffs, it must then be shown that the duty was breached by the failure of exercising an appropriate standard of care. The standard of care owed students is determined by the circumstances. High school chemistry labs are potentially hazardous environments, demanding continuous attention and supervision. Consequently, the science lab teacher owes a higher standard of care due his students. The courts will consider whether the defendant acted as a "reasonable person" would have acted in the same situation. In defining "reasonable person" the courts would consider individuals who have the same (1) physical attributes, (2) normal intelligence, (3) normal perception and memory, and (4) similar skills and knowledge as the defendant (Cambron-McCabe et al., 477). In other words, did Mr. Beaker act as other reasonable and prudent science teachers would have under the same circumstances?

In determining whether Mr. Beaker acted as a reasonable person, courts will consider the fact that as a chemistry teacher, he had superior knowledge as to what could happen if directions were not carefully followed. While schools do not ensure student safety, they must anticipate foreseeable dangers and act or react appropriately to those foreseeable dangers. Mr. Beaker followed the protocol as directed by his department in that he provided students with a legitimate lab handout, and he went over the lab and the MSDS sheets orally and modeled the methodology. He visually inspected that all students had aprons and goggles on before they began their experiments, and while they conducted their lab he circulated the room. What Mr. Beaker failed to do, and should have done knowing the possible harmful consequences, was amend the written lab for the students prior to its distribution. If that was not possible, his next duty was to make sure that each student changed their lab to reflect the appropriate amount of bleach to be used. This could have been done by asking students to repeat his instructions and visually making sure they corrected their papers. Mr. Beaker breached his duty owed his students by failing to exercise an appropriate standard of care, that standard of care being heightened due to the dangerous activity the students were involved in.

Was the negligent conduct the proximate or legal cause of injury?

Plaintiffs must show that the defendant's conduct was the cause of the injury. There are two elements to showing causation: cause-in-fact and proximate or legal cause. A well-known test for cause-in-fact is the but-for test. Under this test the plaintiff must show that the injury would not have occurred "but for" the defendant's conduct (Lane et al., 343). But for the fact that Mr. Beaker failed to change the written directions and consequently the wrong amount of bleach was used, the increased reaction in the container would not have happened and the stopper would not have exploded off the container allowing students to inhale the gas. "In deciding the issue of proximate cause, courts will consider whether the defendant could or should have seen the potentially dangerous consequences of the action" (Lane et al., 343), and again this answer is a definite yes.

Chemistry teachers are quite aware of the potential for dangerous reactions to occur, when even the slightest deviance from the instructions occur. Therefore, their students are foreseeable plaintiffs. In this case, Mr. Beaker's failure to provide proper instructions was the proximate cause of the subsequent injuries to the students.

Did an injury occur?

Even if the above three elements are shown (duty owed, duty breached, proximate cause), there must also be evidence of an actual injury to prevail on a negligence claim. When students are injured in the school setting, school personnel have a duty to provide reasonable assistance that coincides with their training and experience. In this case, no serious or long-term injuries occurred, as supported by a hospital spokesman who stated that they expected the students' symptoms to be cleared up in a few days and no one was "treated" but rather observed and released. When the accident occurred, Mr. Beaker immediately stopped all the experiments. He had one student escorted to the nurses by another student and, after he made arrangements for supervision of the remainder of his classroom, he personally escorted two other students down to the nurses' office. He reported the incident to the nurses as well as the assistant principal, whose office was located next to the nurses' office. He provided the nurses and EMTs with the MSDS sheet. The nurses immediately called poison control and then the rescue squad. The building was immediately evacuated and any students in proximity to the chemical spill were checked out at the school, with a few questionable students transferred to the local hospital. "Where reasonable treatment is provided, no liability will generally be assessed even if the treatment is later proven to be inappropriate" (Cambron-McCabe et al., 481). It is apparent that school and community personnel reacted quickly and effectively to ensure that students were taken care of and not put at further risk.

CONCLUSION

I think Retexe High School dodged a bullet here. While it is obvious that Mr. Beaker was negligent in his conduct, luckily no substantive injuries resulted and therefore legal action was neither pursued nor justified. A negligence claim would not have held up in court in this case. The plaintiffs could have established three of the four elements of negligence (duty owed, duty breached, and proximate cause) but would have failed in showing the fourth criteria, a sufficient injury. It certainly was an incident that could have quickly escalated had Petri, the most severely affected student, had any prior issues of respiratory problems, such as asthma. The students supported Mr. Beaker by initiating and signing a statement saying that it was not his fault but rather the fault of the student that measured incorrectly. The court might well have determined otherwise based on the facts of the case, if it had gone that far. Fortunately, no suits were filed by students or parents and consequently the incident has been forgotten by most. I am sure that C. C. Beaker and I. Goggles are more diligent in their duties, and they certainly should be. A science lab teacher has much more responsibility in the classroom than, say, an English teacher, and should therefore always be crossing his t's and dotting his i's every day in his classroom to ensure the safety of his students. While I agree that no tort liability is supported in this case, I do feel that a written memo to C. C. Beaker and I. Goggles is due from the principal, Mr. Hide, discussing future protocol for lab experiments that are changed to ensure that this type of incident doesn't happen again, and, if it does, the records will show that Mr. Beaker and Mr. Goggles have a prior history of negligence.

REFERENCES

Bailey, Kathleen. 2005. "Chemical Spill at Exeter High School," *Portsmouth Herald*, March 31.

Cambron-McCabe, Nelda, Martha McCarthy, and Stephen Thomas. 2004. *Public school law: Teachers and students rights*. Boston: Pearson.

Lane, Kenneth, Mary Jane Connelly, Julie Mead, Mark Gooden, and Suzanne Eckes. 2005. *The principal's legal handbook*. Dayton: Education Law Association.

Appendix G

Selected Cases for Discussion

ADEQUATE SUPERVISION

Planting Instead of Supervising

A first-grade student fractured her elbow in a fall from the monkey bars. The student was traversing the bars when another student pried her fingers loose, causing her to fall. The two teachers on duty at the time did not witness the fall, and there was some proof that only one of the teachers was "occasionally" monitoring the playground. Instead, they were both involved in planting a garden. One teacher stated "she only turned around from that activity upon hearing the 'uproar' after plaintiff's fall." *Vonungren v. Morris Central School*, 658 N.Y.S.2d 760, 761 (A.D. 3 Dept. 1997).

Mere presence or physical proximity may not be enough to be considered adequate supervision. The educator supervising students must be vigilant and pay attention to those places and situations that have an increased risk of harm, such as monkey bars and other play apparatus. This is especially true when the student activity occurs in places that call for close supervision, such as the chemistry lab, the metal shop, and the swimming pool, and when the activity itself increases the risk of foreseeable danger.

Hall Duty Supervision

A fourth-grade teacher was in the hall supervising the movement of her students from the gymnasium area to the classroom. This was her normal course of conduct. A student was injured in the classroom and lost the sight of one eye while the teacher was in the hallway. There was no history of poor behavior by students while she was briefly out of the room. The teacher was found not to be negligent. *Albers v. Community Consolidated School District No. 204*, 508 N.E.2d 1252 (1987).

How is *Albers* different from *Vonungren*?

The Cheerleader and the Release Form

A sixteen-year-old student was injured in a fall from a pyramid during cheerleading practice. The activity used spotters, but they were unable to catch her or break her fall. The student had participated in cheerleading for four years at the high school level. The student and her father signed a document entitled "Parental Consent, Release from Liability and Indemnity Agreement." The parents sued for negligence.

The court found that the plaintiff's argument that they had not read or understood the release could not prevail absent fraud or duress. It was also established that the voluntary nature of the extracurricular activity furthered a public policy of encouraging athletic programs for youth. The court distinguished a release form for a voluntary nonessential activity from a general release for a compelled activity. Arguably, a release for participation in a required educational activity such as a mandatory field trip may not carry the same weight of indemnity for the school district. *Sharon v. City of Newton*, 769 N.E.2d 738 (Mass. 2002).

The Fight on the Bus

A female elementary school student (eleven years old, four feet tall, 124 pounds) was severely beaten by an older eighth-grade student (six feet tall, 200 pounds) while riding on the school bus. The female student's injuries included a broken clavicle and brain trauma. The bus driver observed the fight but took no other action than to issue a verbal demand to stop fighting. The fight escalated, but the driver failed to stop the bus and return to the school or attempt to stop the fight. The North Carolina Court of Appeals found that the bus driver had opportunities to stop the bus safely before the fight escalated. This failure breached the duty of adequate supervision owed to the injured student. *Simmons v. Columbus County Board of Education*, 615 S.E.2d 69 (N.C.App. 2005).

Injury at the Subway Station

A student was assaulted by another student at a nearby subway station in Brooklyn. The injured student brought suit against the school district, claiming that the school district was negligent because a teacher knew of the impending attack and failed to take appropriate action. The court did not find any admissible evidence that the teacher knew of the impending attack. However, the court wrote, "where a student is injured off school premises generally the school cannot be held liable for the breach of a duty that extends only to the boundaries of school property." The plaintiff student lost. *Bertrand v. Board of Education of City of New York*, 707 N.Y.S.2d 218, 219 (A.D. 2 Dept. 2000).

Red Rover, Red Rover

A student was injured in a game of Red Rover, Red Rover after the game had been specifically prohibited. At the time of the accident there were five teacher aides and one teacher on duty supervising approximately 275 students. The game had only been played for a few moments before the injury occurred, and the supervisors did not have actual or constructive knowledge that the game was in progress. In this case, the court found that the defendants had provided proper supervision. *Toian v. New York City Board of Education*, 519 N.Y.S. 2d 374 (A.D. 2 Dept. 1987).

If the game had progressed for at least five minutes could there have been a different outcome?

Crack-the-Whip

A twelve-year-old boy was killed while playing crack-the-whip on a skateboard after school hours on the school grounds. While the court acknowledged that educators had a duty to supervise students, "[t]o require virtual round-the-clock supervision or prison-tight security for school premises . . . would impose a financial burden which manifestly would impinge on the very educational purpose for which schools exist. . . . [A]t some point the obligation of the public entity to answer for the malfeasance or misfeasance of others, whether children or parents, reaches it outer limits." The plaintiff lost. *Bartell v. Palos Verdes Peninsula School District,* 147 Cal. Rptr. 898, 900 (Cal. Ct.App. 1978).

The Awards Assembly

A grandmother was injured while attending her grandson's award ceremony held in the elementary school's multipurpose room. At the same time and in the same multipurpose room where the ceremony was being conducted a physical education activity was being conducted. The grandmother was knocked over and injured by a student who backed into her while participating in the class activity. The plaintiff grandmother lost her negligent supervision claim, but the court found that there was evidence to support negligence in scheduling the two activities in the same room at the same time. *Pendulik v. E. Hampton Union Free School District,* 792 N.Y.S.2d 583 (N.Y.App. Div. 2d Dept. 2005).

This injury could have been avoided by either rescheduling the awards ceremony or possibly by alerting the physical education teacher to review the lesson and adjust it to meet the foreseeability of injury when active children share the same space with older community members. Unfortunately, it is often the case that we can see clearly after the injury rather than anticipating the likelihood of the injury.

ADEQUATE INSTRUCTIONS

The Mouth Protector

A field hockey coach told his players at the beginning of the season to wear their mouth protectors. A sixteen-year-old student was struck in the mouth with a hockey stick. She was not wearing her mouth protector. The coach failed to remind students to wear their mouth protectors and failed to check to see that the players had their mouth protectors in, which can be readily seen by a quick scan of a player's face. The coach had observed the student for thirty minutes, during which time she did not wear her protector, but took no action. *Baker v. Briarcliff School District,* 613 N.Y.S.2d 660 (A.D. 2 Dept. 1994).

The coach was found negligent. To just give an instruction once is probably not enough if there is an ongoing foreseeable risk of injury.

The Jump

A sixth-grade student was injured when she ran into a wall trying to perform a vertical jump. The jury found the teacher negligent because of his failure to demonstrate the exercise or to provide proper instructions for its safe performance. *Dibortolo v. Metropolitan School District of Washington Township*, 440 N.E.2d 506 (Ind. Ct.App. 1982).

PROPERLY MAINTAINED EQUIPMENT

Water on the Floor

A fifth-grade student slipped and fell in front of his locker as a result of accumulated water on the floor. In order to sustain a slip and fall action against the school district, the plaintiff had to prove that the school district knew that water had accumulated on the floor or the "defect must be visible and apparent and it must exist for a sufficient time prior to the accident to permit defendant's employees to discover and remedy it." *Lottie v. Edwards-Knox Central School District*, 652 N.Y.S.2d 144, 145 (A.D. 3 Dept. 1997).

There was no evidence to show that the principal or members of the faculty or staff had knowledge of any water accumulation. At the trial, they specifically stated that they did not see any water in front of the defendant's locker, nor was there a history of a problem of water accumulation in that spot either from rain or snow.

The Broken Window

A student put his arm through a broken window and was injured. The defendant school district's claim of contributory negligence was not persuasive because the school district had allowed the broken window to go unfixed for four months. The principal either knew or should have known of the broken window and taken appropriate action to reduce the likelihood of injury. This case is distinguished from *Lottie v. Edwards-Knox Central School District* above, in that the broken window was visible and due diligence would have revealed the defect requiring immediate action. *Johnson v. Orleans Parish School Board*, 261 So.2d 699 (1972).

The Drop-off

An elderly grandmother fell down an unmarked step when she walked through a doorway at her granddaughter's school while attending the granddaughter's school concert. She broke her hip. The drop-off was apparent during the day but not necessarily at night. The court held the school district liable due to the unsafe, dangerous condition. *Taney v. Independent School District No. 624*, 673 N.W.2d 497 (Minn. App. 2004).

Courts will routinely award monetary damages to students and invitees who are injured by unsafe conditions or equipment that school authorities should have known of and failed to take the necessary precautions. However, not all injuries at school result in a finding of negligence. The issue of notice or constructive notice of a dangerous condition is important.

WARNINGS REGARDING KNOWN HAZARDS

The Bathroom Visit

A kindergartener was sexually assaulted in the school bathroom by another student with a history of sexually aggressive behavior when the two students visited the bathroom at the same time. The school district was held to be negligent because it failed to warn the substitute teacher of the bathroom pass procedure allowing only one student to use the bathroom at a time. *Miami-Dade County Sch. Board v. A.N. ex rel. A.N.*, 905 So2d 203 (Fla. App. 2005).

Appendix H

Tort Liability Test

Earlier you took a pretest before reading the chapters on tort liability, and you again took the test at the end of chapter 13. Below are the answers for the test and the scores that the principals received by level of the school that they lead.

TRUE or FALSE

1. *TRUE* *Educators owe a legal duty to their students.* Primarily because educators stand in loco parentis to students, they owe them a similar standard of care that parents owe their children.

2. *TRUE* *The reasonable person concept applies to educators under tort liability/negligence.* The acts or inaction of educators will be judged against the reasonable person standard: Would a reasonable and prudent person have acted in the same or a similar manner?

3. *FALSE* *Principals cannot be held liable when a teacher's act or failure to act causes an injury.* Principals who fail to adequately supervise teachers or other employees can be held liable for negligent supervision. Principals owe a duty of reasonable

supervision of employees to students. The breach of that duty that causes an injury can form the basis for liability.

4. FALSE *Proximate cause is a defense in tort liability/negligence cases.* Proximate cause is an element of causation, not a defense. This was the most commonly missed question.

5. *TRUE* *As the foreseeability of injury increases so must the duty owed increase.* If an injury is foreseeable, the duty owed rises to meet the level of danger. For example, in the seashore case study it was foreseeable that the seashore presents a danger to students, therefore the level of supervision owed to the students rises. Working with caustic chemicals, as found in "Ms. Smith's Very Bad Day," elevated the duty owed because it was foreseeable that the chemicals could cause injury. And, in the swing set scenario the swings are a foreseeable danger thus requiring heightened supervision.

6. *TRUE* *Breach of duty is an aspect of the prima facie case in tort liability issues.* The prima facie case consists of duty owed, breach of duty, causation, and sufficient injury.

7. *TRUE* *Sufficient injury or actual loss or injury must be proved in tort liability/negligence cases.* It is the last element (see above) that the plaintiff must prove in establishing a prima facie case. Once the plaintiff has proved the prima facie case, the defendant can assert a defense. If the plaintiff fails to prove the prima facie case, the defendant need not answer.

8. *TRUE* *Adequate/proper supervision is an aspect of the duty educators owe their students.* Educators owe four duties to their students. Adequate supervision is one of the duties. The other three are proper instructions, properly maintained equipment, and provide warnings of known dangers.

9. *FALSE* *All torts involve negligence.* Tort liability involves negligence, intentional torts such as assault and battery, and strict liability. Negligence is one of three torts.

Scores:

Pretest percentage correct _____ Posttest percentage correct _____

1 correct = 11.1%	2 correct = 22.2%	3 correct = 33.3%
4 correct = 44.4%	5 correct = 55.5%	6 correct = 66.7%
7 correct = 77.8%	8 correct = 88.9%	9 correct = 100%

The principals' scores in the DeMitchell and Carroll study are listed below. How do you compare with your level of school and how do you compare with the overall score of the principals?

all: 81.1%; elementary: 78.3% middle: 83.1% high: 81.3%

Appendix I

Court Case: The Toothpick and the Ear

Devin **Fuzie**, an Infant, by Her Mother and Natural Guardian,
Phyllis **Fuzie**, et al.,
v.
South Haven School District No. 30 et al.,
Index No. 86-19805
Supreme Court of New York, Suffolk County
553 N.Y.S.2d 961
March 13, 1990

COUNSEL: *Hammill, O'Brien, Croutier & Dempsey, P. C.,* for defendant. *Lavorata & Conti-Levine* for plaintiffs.

JUDGES: John Copertino, Jr.
OPINION BY: COPERTINO
OPINION: [962] OPINION OF THE COURT

In this negligence action defendant South Haven School District No. 30 (District) moves for summary judgment pursuant to CPLR 3212.

The facts that give rise to this action are not complex. Codefendant Vanessa Bergen, an infant, was a kindergarten student at the South Haven School, one of the District's elementary schools. On October 2,

1980, Vanessa left school with a project assigned by her teacher, Mrs. Paradise, which consisted of toothpicks glued on construction paper. She went directly to the plaintiffs' home from school and arrived at approximately 3:00 P.M.

Devin Fuzie, the two-year-old infant plaintiff, her mother, and Vanessa were sitting in the living room watching television. Plaintiff's mother left them momentarily to go into the kitchen. She heard the plaintiff scream, and when she went back into the living room she found the plaintiff with a toothpick inserted in her ear.

The plaintiffs allege that Vanessa inserted the toothpick into Devin's ear. The plaintiffs contend that defendant District owed the infant plaintiff a duty to exercise reasonable care, and that it breached this duty by failing to supervise the codefendant in the use of the toothpicks. Plaintiffs also contend that a toothpick is a dangerous instrument and, therefore, the school was negligent by entrusting it to its students, specifically codefendant Vanessa Bergen. In addition, plaintiffs allege that the school was negligent in hiring Mrs. Paradise, Vanessa Bergen's teacher.

Because this is a motion for summary judgment the proof of the party opposing the application must be accepted as true and considered in a light most favorable to it *(Museums at Stony Brook v Village of Patchogue Fire Dept.*, 146 AD2d 572). Accordingly, the court will assume that Mrs. Paradise distributed toothpicks to her students, that a project was made with them, and that she allowed her students to leave the school grounds with those projects. The court will also assume that on the day in question one of Mrs. Paradise's students, Vanessa Bergen, went from school to the home of plaintiff Devin Fuzie and inserted one of the toothpicks she had received into plaintiff's ear, causing injury.

Given these circumstances, this application presents three issues of law. The first is whether the defendant District owed any duty of care to a nonstudent injured by a student after school hours and off school grounds. The second is whether a claim of negligence against the District may lie because it entrusted a kindergarten student with a project that consisted of toothpicks. Finally, there is the question of whether [963] the proof submitted can support a claim of negligent hiring.

A school has a duty towards their students to protect them from the negligence of a third party, but this duty is coextensive with physical custody of and control over the child (*Pratt v Robinson*, 39 NY2d 554). The duty arises from the fact that the school has deprived the child of the protection of his parents, and with physical custody comes a duty to exercise the same degree of care as a reasonably prudent parent (*Lawes v Board of Educ.*, 16 NY2d 302). The school's duty to its own charges ceases when the "child has passed out of the orbit of [the school's] authority in such a way that the parent is perfectly free to reassume control over the child's protection" (*Pratt v Robinson, supra*, at 560). However, the school's duty also extends to those persons whose presence on the school grounds is foreseeable, even when school is not in session (*Kush v City of Buffalo*, 59 NY2d 26).

In the present case, the infant plaintiff was not under the physical custody of the defendant. In fact, she was not a student at all. Moreover, she was in her home under the supervision of her mother when the incident occurred, and therefore out of the orbit of the school's authority. Under these circumstances, the court concludes that the District clearly did not owe the infant plaintiff a general duty to protect her from the acts of its student, defendant Vanessa Bergen.

However, this does not resolve the matter. A parent may be liable for injuries to third persons if he or she negligently entrusts a minor with a dangerous instrument (*Nolechek v Gesuale*, 46 NY2d 332) and the school stands in the role of a parent (*Pratt v Robinson, supra*). Whether the defendant was negligent in permitting kindergarten students to work on a class project which involved the use of toothpicks and to allow them to take such projects out of the school without further supervision turns on whether a toothpick may be considered a dangerous instrument. This question has been addressed to a variety of items not ordinarily cast in this role and may be decided by the court (*Koehan v Di Paola*, 97 AD2d 596 [hot pizza not a dangerous instrument]).

Dangerous instruments are those things which in their normal operation are implements of destruction (*Cleary v Maris Co.*, 173 Misc 954), but certain instruments which are not inherently dangerous may become so in the hands of a child (*Young v Dalidowicz*, 92 AD2d 242). Where infants are involved an item may be considered dangerous even when its intended use occurs. A BB gun fired by a three year old (*Masone v Gianotti*, 54 AD2d 269) or a chainsaw operated by a 17 year old (*Bucholtz v Grimmer*, 50 AD2d 1062) constitute foreseeable dangers to third parties. However, riding a skateboard (*Young v Dalidowicz, supra*) and playing on a seesaw (*Pietrzak v McGrath*, 85 AD2d 720) are activities which do not change toys into dangerous instruments.

The court holds that a toothpick's generally intended uses (personal dental hygiene, kitchen tool) are such that it cannot be considered a dangerous instrument. However, under *Nolechk (supra)* and its progeny an object such as a toothpick, not dangerous in itself, may be adjudged a dangerous instrument under certain factual circumstances. The key is foreseeability. In this case, was it foreseeable to Mrs. Paradise that Vanessa Bergen's project would come apart (or be taken apart) and that the component toothpicks would then be handled by the child in such a way that injury to a third person could occur? Because no proof has been adduced tending to show that Vanessa Bergen was anything but an average kindergarten student, the question must be answered in the negative.

A toothpick is of a wholly different character than lawn mowers, BB guns and automobiles, which may be characterized [964] as dangerous in the hands of an infant. To say that a toothpick was a dangerous instrument in the hands of Vanessa Bergen would mean that any number of objects commonly handled by kindergarten-age children would have to be judged dangerous. A sharpened pencil or a pen could cause serious injury if a child pokes another in the ear; so might a crayon if jabbed into an eye; a wire hanger, a ruler or paper clips may do damage if grossly mishandled. Such improper uses might be foreseeable upon some proof that a particular child where known to have had emotional difficulties, rendering misuse of a given instrument a real possibility, but as noted above no such proof is offered here. Indeed, the toothpicks at issue were not sent home loose, but were glued to construction paper. Under these circumstances, the intended use of the toothpicks did not create a foreseeable danger.

Accordingly, the court concludes that the District did not breach any duty of care to the public, including the infant plaintiff, when Mrs. Paradise allowed the toothpicks, glued on paper, to be taken home by her students. Vanessa Bergen's alleged actions were unforeseeable as a matter of law and do not implicate the District.

This ruling moots the claim of negligent hiring, but the court notes that the claim would have failed in any event. To establish liability the plaintiff must prove, *inter alia*, that the employee who caused the injury was unfit for his or her employment (*Annonio v Balzano*, 72 NY2d 806). Absolutely no proof has been adduced or even suggested that Mrs. Paradise was unfit as a teacher. The mere fact that she used toothpicks in a project with her students clearly is inadequate to suggest unfitness, especially in view of the fact that she was implementing a concept learned during her Master's degree training.

Finally, there is a sound policy reason for insulating schools from liability under circumstances such as these. If a teacher—especially those in the lower grades, as here—knew that he or she risked a lawsuit every time an essentially innocuous project was sent home, there very well might be a chilling effect both on innovative approaches to learning and the teacher's attempt to involve the home in the child's education. There are enough problems facing the schools without this kind of unnecessary burden.

The motion is granted.

Questions about the case:

What is the most important thing that you learned from this case?
How did foreseeability impact this case?

About the Authors

Todd A. DeMitchell (B.A., La Verne College; M.A.T., University of La Verne; M.A., University of California, Davis; Ed.D., University of Southern California; Post-Doctorate, Harvard University) spent eighteen years in the public schools as a teacher, assistant principal, principal, director of personnel, and superintendent. Currently, he holds the positions of Kimball Fellow and Professor in the Department of Education and Professor and Coordinator of Graduate Studies in the Justice Studies Program at the University of New Hampshire. He served as program coordinator (Administration and Supervision Program), associate chair, and chair of the Department of Education. In addition, he served as program coordinator and department chair at Sonoma State University. Attorneys have consulted with him regarding negligent supervision of employees and teacher out-of-school behavior.

His research focuses on the legal mechanisms that impact schools and colleges. He coauthored *The Limits of Law-Based School Reform: Vain Hopes and False Promises* with Richard Fossey and *Teacher Unions and TQE: Building Quality Labor Relations* with William A. Streshly, and he has published over 110 articles and book chapters on school law, collective bargaining, and educational policy. His publications have appeared in such journals as *Educational Policy, Education Law Reporter, Journal of Law & Education, School Administrator, Phi Delta Kappan, Journal of School Leadership, Principal, Brigham Young University Education and Law Journal, School Business Affairs,* and the *International Journal of Educational Reform.*

CONTRIBUTING AUTHORS

Sherry Belcher (B.S., *summa cum laude,* University of New Hampshire; M.Ed. University of New Hampshire) is a graduate student in the Certificate of Advanced Graduate Studies Program at the University of New Hampshire. She has taught mathematics at the high school level for seven years.

Terri A. DeMitchell (B.A., with distinction, San Diego State University; J.D., University of San Diego, School of Law; M.A., University of California at Davis; M.Ed., Harvard University) taught elementary school, served as an attorney representing school districts, taught reading methods at the University of New Hampshire, and is a children's author for middle level readers (*You Will Come Back,* Mayhaven Award Winner). She has published articles on educational malpractice, teacher out-of-school behavior, and school library censorship.

David J. Hebert (B.A., University of Maine; M.Ed., Duquesne University; Ph.D., Kent State University) is completing his thirty-ninth year as a faculty member at the University of New Hampshire. Currently, he holds the position of Professor in the Department of Education's Graduate Program in Counseling. A few years ago the university honored him with the Brierley Award. This award is presented yearly to one university faculty member for excellence in teaching. In addition, he is a licensed psychologist; he maintained a part-time private practice as a psychotherapist for over twenty-five years, and has been a consultant psychologist for a wide range of agencies and schools. His research has been published in *Perceptual and Motor Skills, Journal of Psychiatric Nursing and Mental Health Services, Psychological Reports, Educational and Psychological Measurement, Journal of Applied Rehabilitation Counseling, Journal of Counseling and Development, The Clinical Supervisor,* and the *Journal of Mental Health Counseling*

Christian M. Keiner (B.A., with high honors, University of California, Santa Barbara; J.D. with distinction, University of the Pacific, McGeorge School of Law) is Of Counsel to Kronick, Moskovitz, Tiedemann & Girard in Sacramento, California. He has practiced education law for twenty-five years.

www.ingramcontent.com/pod-product-compliance
Ingram Content Group UK Ltd.
Pitfield, Milton Keynes, MK11 3LW, UK
UKHW012034150926
475560UK00001B/4

9 781578 865000